God, Immortality, Ethics

God, Immortality, Ethics: A Concise Introduction to Philosophy

DOUGLAS P. LACKEY

Baruch College and the Graduate Center
City University of New York

Wadsworth Publishing Company
Belmont, California
A Division of Wadsworth, Inc.

Philosophy Editor: Kenneth King
Editorial Assistant: Michelle Palacio
Production: Cece Munson, The Cooper Company
Print Buyer: Randy Hurst
Interior Designer: MaryEllen Podgorski
Cover Designer: Cynthia Bassett
Cover Art: SCALA/ART RESOURCE, N.Y. Detail from *School of Athens* by Raphael
Copy Editor: Phyllis Cairns
Compositor: Bi-Comp, Inc.
Signing Representative: Eileen Corcoran

Printed in the United States of America

1 2 3 4 5 6 7 8 9 10---94 93 92 91 90

Library of Congress Cataloging-in-Publication Data

Lackey, Douglas P.
    God, Immortality, Ethics: A Concise Introduction to Philosophy /
Douglas P. Lackey.
        p.   cm.
    Includes bibliographies and index.
    ISBN 0-534-12042-3
    1. Philosophy—Introductions.   2. God—Proof.   3. Future life.
4. Ethics.   I. Title.
BD21.L19 1989
100—dc20   89-14699
                                                           CIP

For Milton Munitz

Contents

Preface

This book is the result of a long struggle with a problem that faces almost all professors of philosophy: how to introduce students to the subject.

The standard options are all frustrating. If the instructor assigns classic historical works, the student gets only a limited picture of contemporary attitudes and spends weeks struggling with arguments that are often so bad that any contemporary graduate student in philosophy would be embarrassed to express them. If the instructor uses a textbook written by a single contemporary author, the student obtains current views, but is blocked from appreciating that a book of philosophy can be a work of enduring genius. If the instructor switches to an anthology of classic excerpts, he or she bewilders the student with multiple prose styles and clashing technical vocabularies.

One source of the trouble is that philosophy has a problem relating to its own history. Because philosophy is a rational discipline, informed by mathematics and science and historical events, many of the positions and arguments presented by classic philosophers have become obsolete, or at least require revision in the light of later discoveries. At the same time, books of philosophy are often great works of literature and have the timeless value of works of art. There is no problem in the history of philosophy—causation, freedom, the powers of God, the nature of theoretical entities—that cannot be discussed with more depth and rigor by philosophers in the 1990s than by any philosopher in ages past. But there are few pages of contemporary philosophy that exhibit the philosophic genius of a page of Plato or Aristotle or Kant or Hegel.*

The trick is to expose the student to the results of contemporary philosophy *and* the achievements of the past. One blunt but effective solution is simply

---

* There are *some* contemporary philosophical classics. One work of dazzling genius is Ludwig Wittgenstein's *Philosophical Investigations* (Cambridge: Cambridge University Press, 1953). Among more recent works, I would suggest *Naming and Necessity* (Cambridge, Mass.: Harvard University Press, 1982) by Saul Kripke, and *Reasons and Persons* (New York: Oxford University Press, 1984) by Derek Parfit.

to assign one contemporary book *and* some classic texts. Since academic terms are short and students are busy, the contemporary book and the classic texts had best be brief. I have tried here to supply a concise contemporary book: a review of three basic problems showing what philosophers think about these issues today. The classic texts are at the instructor's choice. For myself, I have found nothing better than some of the shorter Platonic dialogues.

I am grateful to Louis Pojman, University of Mississippi, and Raymond Martin, University of Maryland, for comments on earlier drafts. This book is dedicated to Milton Munitz, professor emeritus of philosophy at Baruch College and the Graduate Center of the City University of New York, who in a lifetime of work in philosophy has never deviated from the deep questions or lost sight of the big picture.

Introduction

In the palace of the Vatican, a few steps from Michelangelo's Sistine Chapel, are rooms decorated with frescoes by Raphael. In the greatest of these frescoes, *The School of Athens* (1510), Raphael shows the great thinkers of ancient Greece: the Pythagoreans at work on arithmetic; the Euclideans drawing geometrical proofs; Heraclitus, Socrates, Diogenes, Epicurus, and other famous philosophers. In the center of the fresco stand Plato and Aristotle. Carrying a copy of his *Timaeus,* which contains his theory of the universe, Plato points upward to the divine heavens for inspiration. Holding a copy of his *Ethics,* Aristotle dissents, gesturing to the surrounding human world as the source of knowledge. In the background, dozens of other philosophers are involved in animated discussions.

I believe that Raphael in this painting caught the spirit of philosophy and provided a model for this book. I begin with divine subjects—God and the soul—and end with the human world and human ethical problems. Like Raphael, I have tried to exhibit an essential connection between work in philosophy and developments in science. Most of all, I have tried to show that philosophy is a social activity consisting essentially of discussion, disagreement, and argument.

Even people who know very little about philosophy know philosophers love to argue. So it should come as no surprise that this philosophical book is crammed with arguments, arguments for and against the existence of God, the soul, free will, and a universal and objective moral code. These are not the only issues in philosophy, but for me they are the most interesting ones, and every problem in philosophy can be touched in the course of considering them.

My presentation takes the form of debates, with arguments pro and con regarding each issue, followed by criticisms and rebuttals. In each case, I have stated the arguments as forcefully as I can, just as if I believed them myself; then I have stated the rebuttals as forcefully as I can, just as if I believed them myself. Thus, though this book has a single author, it speaks with many voices. When going through the debates, the reader should beware of taking any section or any paragraph as the author's last word on the subject.

This proliferation of arguments may frustrate some readers who want to "get to the point," skipping over the discussion. But in philosophy, the discussion, not the conclusion, is often itself the main point. On each issue, I have tried to balance the arguments pro and con, leaving readers free to draw their own conclusions. No definite verdict is reached about the existence of God or any other subject. This, too, is characteristic of philosophy: all its main questions remain unsettled. This lack of results is not a weakness in philosophy, but simply a matter of definition. Whenever something is definitely settled, we stop calling it philosophy and call it science.

Science has taken much from philosophy, and in return science can do much to illuminate philosophical discussions. For this reason, I have included a number of accounts of contemporary scientific theories. I have also included a number of discussions of religious doctrines: Jewish, Christian, Hindu, and Buddhist. Philosophy has its own territory, but that territory lies somewhere between science and religion. Indeed, one task of this book is to determine how much religious hope the scientific attitude can tolerate.

The Existence of God

The Judeo-Christian-Islamic Conception of God

Different religions have different conceptions of God, but in Part I we will concentrate on the idea of God as it has been developed in Judaism, Christianity, and Islam. For Western readers, this is the most familiar conception of God, and the God of these religions is a God that perhaps a third of the world's population believes to exist.

According to these religions, God is an *all-powerful, all-good being.* These properties of possessing supreme power and supreme goodness are basic properties of God, neither of which can be deduced from the other. But from these two basic and independent properties of God, other properties can be deduced.

From the postulate that God is all-powerful (or "omnipotent"), we can deduce that God is *immortal,* which means that God never dies, and *eternal,* which means that God is outside time and does not grow older as time marches on. Obviously a being that is all-powerful should not be subject to birth or death, or limited by the flow of time. From the postulate that God is all-powerful, it also follows that God is *immaterial,* that is, not composed of atoms and molecules or matter that occupy space (since any object composed of matter might some day disintegrate). Perhaps most importantly, from the postulate that God is all-powerful, it follows that God is *unique.* There cannot be two all-powerful beings, since each would be subject to the other, and hence not truly all-powerful.

If God is all-powerful, God must be able to do everything that can be done. Among the things God must be able to do are thinking and knowing. Thus, God is *all-knowing,* possessing life and consciousness and perception and knowledge. From this idea that God is all-knowing (or "omniscient") it follows that

God is a *person,* not an abstract principle or an unthinking cosmic force. Perhaps it is this idea that God is a person that the Hebrew Bible refers to when it says that human beings were created "in the image of God" (Genesis 1:26).

From the postulate that God is *supremely good,* it follows that God possesses every good quality and all good things flow from God. Thus, God is, according to these faiths, *supremely and uniquely worthy of worship.* It also follows from God's goodness that all of God's actions are *morally right.* Furthermore, since we can attribute moral qualities to God's actions, we must believe that God has *free will,* since persons can make moral choices only if they have free will.

The properties of being all-powerful and all-good are *essential* properties of God: anything that is *not* all-powerful or *not* all-good could not be God. If God exists, He also possessess many *nonessential* properties. A nonessential property of God is a property such that God could lack it and still be God. *Creator of the Heavens and the Earth,* though truly a property of God according to the Bible and the Koran, is a nonessential property of God. If God has free will, God could have chosen not to create the universe. In that case, God would not be the Creator, but God would still be God.

The Question of Existence

Given the previous analysis of the *concept* of God, we know many truths about God. In particular, we know that if God exists, God is powerful, and that if God exists, God is good. Despite our knowledge of these hypothetical truths, we do not yet know *whether God exists,* whether in fact there exists any being who *is* all-powerful and all-good.

The statement "God is good" is true by definition, and we know that it is true simply by knowing the meaning of the word "God." (It amounts to saying "an all-good being is good.") But the claim "God exists" is not true by definition. It is a claim that something exists, different from the mere concept of God, that has the properties of being all-powerful and all-good. This assertion that God exists is commonly called *theism,* and the opposing assertion that God does not exist is called *atheism.*

Paying attention to the difference between *God* and *the concept of God* will prevent certain mistakes that sceptical persons make when they criticize religious belief. For example, sceptics commonly assert, "God is just an idea in people's minds." But this cannot be true. God, if God exists, exists everywhere, not just in people's minds. What exists in people's minds is just the *concept* of God.

Why the Existence of God Is Important

Some people, even persons who believe in God, think that the existence of God is an abstruse subject, far removed from the real business of life. In their view, life should be pretty much the same whether God exists or not. Given the definition of God as an all-powerful, all-good being, however, the idea that God's existence *doesn't matter* is implausible.

If God exists, then all our actions are seen and judged. If there is no God, then many of our actions go unseen and unjudged. If God exists, every event in our lives, every event in everyone's life, has a meaning because it is part of God's plan, even if that plan is unknown to us. If God does not exist, the existence of the human race is meaningless, in the sense that its existence is not part of anyone's plan or purpose.

Even more significantly, if God exists, good will ultimately triumph over evil. All decent people are frustrated by the worldly success of mean and unscrupulous individuals. Nevertheless, the theist is consoled by the thought that, since God exists, the success of the wicked is only temporary. The atheist, contemplating the success of the wicked, must live with the thought that the wicked may forever get away with their crimes. Theists live in a world of divine justice and divine meaning. Atheists live in a world of irregular justice, in which the meaning of events is supplied only by themselves and their fellow human beings. The theist and the atheist live in different mental and emotional universes.

Believing "on Faith"

The philosopher is interested in arguments for and against the existence of God. For many religious believers, arguments for and against God's existence are irrelevant, since they believe in God "on faith," without reasons. Certainly it is possible to believe in God without having any arguments for God's existence. Indeed, for many religious people it is irreverent and imprudent to raise questions about the existence of God. So why bother about the arguments?

One reason for bothering about arguments for God's existence is that without arguments one cannot truly say that one *knows* God exists. There is such a thing as *believing* on faith, but there is no such thing as *knowing* on faith. To know something one must have good reasons to back up one's belief, and to believe on faith is to believe without reasons. But does the difference between *merely believing* that God exists and *knowing* that God exists have religious significance?

Suppose that God does exist. Isn't it a greater act of piety to *know* this fact rather than merely believe it? Wouldn't it be odd of God to create human beings with a capacity for rational thought while demanding that they not use this capacity to think about their creator? If so, it cannot be irreverent or imprudent to inquire into the evidence for the existence of God. Perhaps this is why most varieties of Judaism, Christianity, and Islam maintain that God's existence is something that *can* be proved by human reason. Belief on faith is sufficient, but not necessary, for living a religious life.

First Argument for Belief: Pascal's Wager

Our first argument for God's existence was invented in the seventeenth century by a French philosopher, Blaise Pascal (1623–1662). It is known as Pascal's Wager.

In Pascal's argument, the decision to believe or not believe in God is treated as a bet that a person may win or lose. If I believe in God and God exists, I win; if I believe in God and God does not exist, I lose. Similarly, if I *don't* believe in God and God does *not* exist, I win; if I don't believe in God and God exists, I lose. Is belief in God a rational bet?

For Pascal, the answer is found by considering what I win or lose in each case. Pascal argued that if I believe in God and God exists, God will reward my faith with heavenly salvation; if I don't believe in God and God exists, God will punish my atheism with eternal hellfire. On the other hand, if I believe in God and God does not exist, I lose the effort and expense of church membership; if I don't believe in God and God does not exist, I gain nothing beyond the intellectual satisfaction of being right. This information can be expressed in a diagram as follows:

	God exists	God doesn't exist
Belief	Salvation	Small expense
Nonbelief	Hellfire	Small reward

Looking at the payoffs, it is clear that I run a great risk by not believing in God, but I only run a small risk by believing in God. Thus, it would not be rational to reject belief in God unless we were absolutely sure that God does not exist. But we cannot be sure that God does not exist. The most rational bet, said Pascal, is to believe in God.

Criticism of Pascal's Wager

Pascal's argument assumes that God will provide rewards for those who believe in God and punishments for those who do not. This is commonly assumed by religious believers, but one can question whether this is true.

Suppose that Atheist Alex and Believer Barnabas arrive in heaven at the same time. God *might* pass judgment as follows:

Though I exist, I have provided human beings with very little evidence for My existence. Alex used the tool of reason that I have given to humanity and deduced from this lack of evidence that I do not exist. Barnabas abused my gift of reason by believing in Me without evidence. I will reward the atheist for respecting My gifts, but not the believer who abused them.

Furthermore, suppose that for his whole life Believer Barnabas has broken every moral law, and Atheist Alex has lived an exemplary moral life. Is it so obvious that God will save Barnabas and condemn Alex simply because Barnabas believed in God and Alex did not?

There is an even deeper problem with Pascal's argument. In Pascal's view, religious believers should believe because they hope they will be rewarded for their belief. But there is something mercenary about believing in God *for the purpose of* being rewarded. Indeed, it seems unlikely that God will reward believers who believe in Him *only* to get to heaven.

Pascal's Wager Revised

It is possible to revise Pascal's argument so that it does not rely on assumptions about rewards and punishments in the next life. Religious belief provides rewards to believers in *this* life by supplying emotional resources that would not be there in the absence of belief. People who have suffered some personal tragedy often remark that religious belief "got them through" their time of trouble. If I believe in God, I am rewarded with the consolation religious belief provides, whether God exists or not. If I do not believe in God, I receive no particular reward, whether God exists or not. We have a new diagram:

	God exists	God doesn't exist
Belief	Valuable consolation	Valuable consolation
Nonbelief	Unjustified despair	Justified despair

This argument is even stronger than Pascal's original argument. It shows it is rational to believe in God even if it is *certain* that God does not exist.

Criticism of the Revised Wager

The revised version of Pascal's Wager assumes that belief in God provides rewards for believers even when God does not exist. But what, precisely, are these rewards if God does not exist?

Suppose that Susan's mother dies, and Susan believes her mother is now "with God." This belief consoles her. But now suppose there is no God. It follows that Susan's mother cannot be with God. Is Susan really better off for having this false but consoling belief?

Some philosophers would argue that having a false belief is itself a kind of harm. Suppose, for example, a machine is invented that broadcasts movies directly into a person's brain, so subtly that the person receiving the movie believes he is actually living in the film. For a $100,000 fee the Dream Machine Corporation will broadcast directly into your brain a movie in which *you* are the star. For a $1 million fee they will broadcast into your brain a *lifelong* movie, in which every fantasy and aspiration you ever had will be fulfilled in spades—and you die without ever knowing the dream is a fake. If you had $1 million, would you buy the Perfect Lifelong Dream? Many people would not because they will (regretfully) concede that the satisfaction of believing their hopes are fulfilled has little value when the satisfaction is a delusion. If you have fantasized winning the Nobel Prize, it is *winning the prize* that you value, not *dreaming* you are winning the prize. The Perfect Lifelong Dream does *not* give you what you want. It only makes you believe you have what you want.

Now, the consolations and satisfactions of the Perfect Lifelong Dream are as good and as long lasting as the consolations that belief in God provides Susan. If there is no value in the Perfect Lifelong Dream, then there is no value in Susan's consolations either, if there is no God. It follows that the revised Pascal's Wager is mistaken when it assumes rewards should be assigned for the box Belief/God doesn't exist. It seems theism can provide true consolation only if theism itself is true.

Second Argument for Belief: The Ontological Argument

The ontological argument was invented in the late eleventh century by St. Anselm (1033–1109), who was England's Archbishop of Canterbury. Anselm stated the argument in a very complicated form; but in the seventeenth century, the French philosopher Rene Descartes (1596–1650) recognized that the proof can be stated much more simply. His simple version of the argument is

1. God possesses every perfection (Premise);

2. Existence is a perfection (Premise);

3. God possesses existence (Conclusion).

What the ontological argument is driving at is this. God is supposed to be a supremely perfect being. But a supremely perfect being must have everything it needs in order to be perfect. Existence is one of the things a perfect being needs in order to be perfect. So God must have existence.

It should be obvious that the premises in this argument are logically connected to its conclusion. *If* it is true that God possesses every perfection, and *if* existence is a perfection, then God *must* possess existence. Such arguments are called *logically valid*. But a logically valid argument like this proves its conclusion only if its premises are true. Are they?

The first premise says God possesses every perfection. This follows directly from the fact that God is all-good. The first premise is true by definition.

The second premise says existence is a perfection. What this means is that existence is a property that is good for a thing to have. The reader might object that this is not true for things like flies and viruses. But certainly, for a given fly, it is better *from the fly's standpoint* that it exists than that it does not exist. For flies, the existence of flies is a good thing.

The statement "existence is a perfection" implies that nonexistence is a defect. Suppose a salesman told you he had a fabulous car on sale that seats six, gets ninety miles a gallon, reaches sixty miles per hour in five seconds flat, but has one small defect—it lacks existence! You might agree that the nonexistence of the car is indeed a defect. This shows that existence is indeed a perfection. Both premises of the argument are true, and the conclusion is proven.

Criticism of the Ontological Argument

Gaunilo's Objection to the Ontological Argument. After Anselm worked out the ontological argument, he had the argument copied and distributed. Gaunilo, a monk in France, studied the argument and raised an objection. Gaunilo argued that if the ontological argument were a sound argument, the pattern of the argument could be used to prove the existence of all kinds of perfect things. Gaunilo argued, for example, that if Anselm's argument were sound the following argument would be sound:

1. A perfect island possesses every perfection;

2. Existence is a perfection; therefore,

3. A perfect island possesses existence.

Gaunilo, of course, did not believe that perfect islands exist; but he did believe that this argument is as logically valid as Anselm's: its conclusion is logically connected to its premises. Furthermore, the first premise of the argument is true—true by definition. It must be, then, that the second premise is false. (When a valid argument has a false conclusion at least one of its premises must be false.) So Anselm was just wrong when he asserted that "existence is a perfection."

Kant's Objection to the Ontological Argument. In the late eighteenth century, the great German philosopher Immanuel Kant (1724–1804) raised a different objection to Anselm's argument. Anselm had assumed that existence was a property that things possessed, a property like their size or shape. But Kant argued that existence is not a property like size or shape, since it is not a property of things at all.

What is existence, if it is not a property of things? One thing we might say is this: the existence of a thing is *the thing itself.* The proof of this is that if you subtract existence from a thing, the result is not *that thing* minus existence: the result is *nothing* whatsoever. For example, an ideal car, minus existence, is not a car with a defect. It is not even a car; it is simply nothing.

If existence is not a property of things, then *nonexistence* is not a property of things either. It follows that there are no nonexistent things. At first sight, this conclusion seems paradoxical: what about Santa Claus, Goldilocks, and the Three Little Pigs. Aren't they truly nonexistent things?

The British philosopher Bertrand Russell (1872–1970), developing Kant's line of thought, argued that they are not. Russell agreed, of course, that Santa Claus does not exist, but he denied that Santa Claus is a nonexistent thing. When we say "Santa Claus does not exist," we are asserting that "there is no man at the North Pole who wears a red suit, makes toys, and drives reindeer." We are *not* saying that "there is a nonexistent man at the North Pole who wears a red suit, makes toys, and flies reindeer." This may seem like splitting hairs. But if Kant and Russell are right about the nature of existence, existence is not a perfection and the ontological argument is unsound.

Third Argument for Belief:
The Cosmological Argument

Pascal's Wager and the ontological argument are very abstract arguments, much loved by philosophers but not very popular with ordinary people. Perhaps the most popular argument for God for the ordinary person is the cosmological argument—the argument that God must exist because only God could have created the universe. In outline the cosmological argument reads:

1. The universe had a beginning in time (Premise 1);

2. Everything that has a beginning in time must have a cause (Premise 2); so,

3. There exists a cause of the universe; and

4. The cause of the universe could only be God (Premise 3); so,

5. God exists.

God, in short, is the first cause of everything in the physical universe.

Premise 1. The first premise of the cosmological argument—that the universe had a beginning in time—implies that the physical history of the universe does not stretch infinitely far into the past. For people accustomed to the story of the Book of Genesis, nothing could be more natural than thinking that there was some moment at which the universe *began.* But many eminent philosophers, Aristotle (384–322 B.C.) for example, have thought that the idea of a beginning of the universe is absurd (because "nothing can come from nothing"). Thus, Aristotle believed that the universe had no beginning and that the past history of the universe is infinite. Is there any evidence that the past history of the universe is *finite*?

Evidence that the universe *does* have a beginning has been provided in recent years by the branch of astronomy called *cosmology*. The data from cosmology are worth describing in detail.

In the 1920s, astronomers established for the first time that certain fuzzy patterns of light in the sky were actually large clusters of stars, or galaxies, located at distances from Earth far greater than the distances of the stars in the night sky. The stars in the night sky, in fact, were themselves part of the Milky Way, a local galaxy, the center of which is visible as a filmy streak in the night sky in summer.

In the 1930s, astronomers discovered that the light from the galaxies was shifted toward the red, that is, the frequencies of light obtained from the stars in distant galaxies were lower than one would expect if those galaxies were stationary relative to the earth. There are various explanations of this Red Shift, but the one that made the most scientific sense was that the galaxies are all moving away from the earth. More precisely (since the earth is not at the center of the universe), the Red Shift shows that the average distance between the galaxies is increasing with time.

Now, if the average distance between the galaxies is increasing as time goes on, it follows that if we go *backward* in time, the average distance between the galaxies is *decreasing*. If we could put the history of the universe on film and then run the film backward, we would see the galaxies all converging in a small volume of space. By the late 1940s, various astronomers were suggesting the expansion of the universe from the past to the present was caused by a gigantic explosion, named the Big Bang, which hurled the matter of the galaxies outward in all directions. In 1966, evidence for the existence of the Big Bang was discovered in background radiation evenly distributed throughout the universe—the residual heat of the early great explosion.

In the astronomy of the 1960s, there was no theory as to what the matter of the universe was doing during or before the Big Bang. For all cosmology knew, the matter of the universe could have been in a tight ball for eons and then suddenly exploded. In short, the Big Bang theory of the 1960s was at least *compatible* with the idea that the physical universe is infinitely old.

In the early 1970s, physicists Steven Hawking and Roger Penrose proved that the matter of the present universe could *not* be infinitely old. They demonstrated—if you imagine time running backward once again—that as the galaxies approached one another in the distant past, they came together into a single dense ball. The great forces acting inside this ball broke down the normal resistance of matter to compression, so the ball steadily became denser and denser. At one point in the past, all the matter of our universe was compressed into an object the size of a basketball; still earlier, the size of a golf ball. If we look at still earlier and earlier moments, at one projected point in the past, the density of the universe is infinite and its volume is zero. This hypothetical moment of infinite density is located by astronomers between 10 and 20 billion years B.C.

Contemporary Big Bang theory, then, does not merely say that the *galaxies* are not more than 20 billion years old. It says that the matter and energy *of which the galaxies are made* are not more than 20 billion years old.

What was going on before the Big Bang? According to Einstein's General Theory of Relativity, developed as a theory of gravity in 1915 and applied by Einstein to cosmology in 1917, nothing whatsoever, not even time. In the General Theory, space and time are *features of* the physical universe, not dimensions that *contain* the universe. The universe is all there is of space and time, and the beginning of the Big Bang is the beginning of time itself. There are no moments of time before the Big Bang, and nothing has ever happened that should be dated before the Big Bang. If this theory is right, then the cosmological argument is correct in saying that the universe has a beginning in time.

Premise 2. The claim that *everything with a beginning in time must have a cause* is called the Law of Universal Causation or the Principle of Sufficient Reason. As the German philosopher Gottfried Leibniz (1646–1716) explained it, if there is no cause that makes something happen, then nothing will happen, because "nothing is simpler and easier than something." The law applies to all events, so it applies to the Big Bang. Unless there was something that made the Big Bang happen, it never would have happened at all.

Why should we believe the Law of Universal Causation? To begin with, we already know that a great many events do have causes because we know what these causes are. The remaining events either have *unknown* causes or have *no causes at all*. Take any such event: should we assume that it has no cause or that we simply don't known what its cause is?

Many times in the past, when people have assumed that an event E has no cause, science has eventually discovered the cause of E. We can prove events have causes, but we can never prove an event has no cause, since we can never be sure what the future science will be able to explain. For any event E for which no cause is proven, it is always more reasonable to assume that E has a real but unknown cause than that E has no cause.

Another argument for the Law of Universal Causation comes from Immanuel Kant. Kant wondered how it was possible, in general, to distinguish perceptions of the real world from other sorts of perceptions, like hallucinations, which provide no knowledge of the world at all. He argued that the Law of Universal Causation was a tool we must use in order to distinguish genuine experiences from nongenuine ones. Genuine experiences are experiences of objects *connected to* other objects by relations of cause and effect. Hallucinations are experiences of objects *not* connected to other objects by relations of cause and effect. Thus, any event that has no causes is something we would have to classify as *unreal*. Because of the way we must think about the world when we know anything about it, the Law of Universal Causation applies to all worldly events.

Premise 3. Even if we have established that the Big Bang must have a cause, we still must show what the first cause is. We cannot simply assume that the Creator of the universe is God, since Creator of the Heavens and the Earth is not an essential property of God. To show that the Creator is God, we must show that the Creator is all-powerful and all-good.

Obviously, any creator of the universe must have great power. But why should we think the Creator is *all*-powerful? Why can't we just say the Creator is *very* powerful but not *all*-powerful? One reason might be that any being who is powerful enough to create a universe is powerful enough to do anything at all. Notice that the cause of the universe has created matter and energy from nothing, or at least from something that is not itself matter and energy. It seems reasonable to think a being who could create matter and energy from nothing could do anything whatsoever.

Why should we think the Creator of the universe is supremely good? One reason is that if the Creator is the cause of all things, then all good things come from the Creator. Furthermore, the Creator could have chosen not to create these good things. It follows that the Creator must have wanted to create them, and his desire to create what is good shows that the Creator *is* good. But since the Creator is all-powerful, his desire to create the good knows no bounds. He will create an infinite amount of good, and thereby show that He is infinitely good.

Thus, the Creator, infinitely powerful and infinitely good, must be none other than God.

Criticism of the Cosmological Argument

The Universe Might Have Begun Spontaneously. It would not be wise for critics of the cosmological argument to challenge the Big Bang theory that supports the first premise of the argument. Though a few cosmologists reject the theory, most think the evidence in its favor is overwhelming. The point to attack in the cosmological argument is the point at which it claims the universe must have a cause. The critic can argue the Big Bang was an event that had no cause at all. It happened spontaneously, without cause.

If we say this, we are rejecting the Law of Universal Causation. But many philosophers and many scientists believe the Law of Universal Causation is false. The reason lies in the theory of *quantum physics,* the physics developed between 1900 and 1930 by Max Planck, Albert Einstein, Nils Bohr, Louis de Broglie, Werner Heisenberg, Erwin Schrodinger, Paul Dirac, and others to explain the behavior of the tiniest bits of matter and energy. According to quantum physics, the behavior of atomic particles is not determined precisely by prior conditions. It is to some degree spontaneous. For example, it is not possible to predict when a given radioactive atom will decay, and this difficulty in prediction is not due to our ignorance of the atom. It springs from the nature of the atom itself.

Thus, the Law of Universal Causation is rejected in quantum physics. Some events don't have causes. But perhaps the Law of Universal Causation only fails for little things like radioactive atoms. Can we say that the law also fails for the Big Bang, and that the creation of the universe was as spontaneous an event as the decay of a radioactive atom?

There are two reasons for thinking the Law of Universal Causation fails for the Big Bang. First, the Law of Universal Causation says that every event has a cause, and this means that every event has a cause *that is another earlier event*. Since the Big Bang is the first moment of time, nothing can be earlier than it. Second, according to Big Bang cosmology, at some past point in time the entire universe was no larger than an atomic particle. Whatever rules apply to atomic particles would apply to the universe at that time. The behavior of a universe of such small size could be as spontaneous as the decay of a radioactive atom.

So the big bang might have no cause. How then did it happen? One explanation provided by quantum theory depends on the fact that in quantum physics the energy levels of particles and systems can never be precisely measured, but oscillate spontaneously between certain levels. For the smallest particles, this oscillation between energy levels may cause the energy level to drop to zero, at which point the particle ceases to exist. Conversely, the oscillation can raise a particle from zero to some finite level; that is, it brings a particle into existence. Such particles, usually called virtual particles, are literally coming into existence from a vacuum, that is, from nothing. A few physicists, Heinz Pagels for one, have suggested that one could explain the Big Bang as a fluctuation in a vacuum, like the fluctuations that bring virtual particles into existence. But if the fluctuations are spontaneous, then the creation of the universe from a vacuum is also spontaneous.

The Creator Might Not Be God. Suppose the preceding objection is mistaken and the universe does indeed have a cause. All we know about this cause is that it has the power to create our universe. This is far from showing that the Creator of the universe is all-powerful. An all-powerful being must be able to create an infinite number of universes. We cannot tell, if a being has made one universe, whether it has the power to create any more. For all we know, the Creator of the universe might have died in the effort of making it.

There is still less reason to think that the Creator of the universe *must* be all-good. If one argues that all good things come from the Creator, then one must argue that all bad things come from the Creator as well. But bad things cannot come from a supremely good being. Even if the universe has a Creator, the fact of creation is not sufficient to show that this Creator must be God.

Fourth Argument for Belief: The Argument from Contingency

The cosmological argument takes as its starting point the creation of the universe in the distant past. As we have seen, sceptics object that this argument cannot show that the Creator of the universe still exists in the present. The argument from contingency avoids this difficulty by taking as its starting point the *present* existence of the universe. It asserts that without God there is no reason why the universe should exist *right now*. The cosmological argument leads to God as the Creator of the universe in the past. The argument from contingency leads to God as the Sustainer of the universe in the present. The argument says:

1.   The universe exists and is a contingent being (Premise 1);

2.   Contingent beings exist only if a necessary being exists (Premise 2); so,

3.   A necessary being exists; and

4.   Necessary beings are all-powerful and all-good (Premise 3); so,

5.   God exists.

Premise 1. A being is said to be *contingent* if it is possible for that being never to have existed. Each human being, for example, is a contingent entity, because the parents of that human being might not have met. In fact, everything in the universe is a contingent entity, which prompts one to believe that the whole universe is a contingent entity as well.

In the preceding section, we considered two views about the origins of the universe. Either the universe came into existence by an act of God, or it came into existence spontaneously, without cause. Either way, the universe is contingent. If God created it, it might not have existed since God might have chosen not to create it. If it came into existence by chance, then by chance it might not have come into existence.

Premise 2. Consider a certain Mr. Jones. Since he is contingent, he might never have existed. So we can ask: Why does he exist? Since he exists, there must be *some* explanation of his existence. Suppose we say, "Jones exists because of his parents." That does not *fully* explain why Jones exists, because Jones's parents are contingent beings and we need to know why *they* exist. (Obviously we are not getting anywhere if we explain Jones's parents by pointing to his grandparents.) We cannot fully explain any contingent being by referring to other contingent beings. We can fully explain contingent beings only by getting back to a necessary being, a being that could not possibly fail to exist, a being that exists because it is its nature to exist. When we come up against a necessary being, our questions come to an end. It makes no more sense to ask why a necessary being exists than to ask why a circle is round.

Contingent beings are explained by necessary beings. But necessary beings do more than *explain* contingent beings: they keep them in existence. As Mr. Jones persists from moment to moment, certain of his qualities stay relatively unchanged: his genetic code, his fingerprints, and so forth. By itself, the universe might change constantly, wiping out all these continuities, without which there would be no Mr. Jones. The reason for the continuities must be found in something that does not change because it has to be the way it is. This Sustainer of all contingent things is the necessary being that explains them all.

Premise 3. If the contingent beings of the universe depend on a necessary being, that being is the Sustainer of the universe. As with the Creator, we can ask whether the Sustainer of the universe must be God.

The answer can be found by considering the relationship between the Sustainer and what He sustains. That contingent beings persist from moment to moment depends on a necessary being who supplies contingent things with the continuity they need to be what they are. So we can say that the necessary being is the *substance*, the very existence, of all contingent beings. So, wherever there is power, the necessary being is the very substance of that power: it is what makes power powerful. Likewise, wherever goodness exists, the necessary being is the very substance of that goodness: it is what makes goodness good. For this reason, we should say that the Sustainer is supremely good and supremely powerful. As the thirteenth-century philosopher and theologian Thomas Aquinas (1224–1274) put it, God is *not* all-powerful in the sense of having the highest degree of power, *not* all-good in the sense of having the highest degree of goodness. He is all-powerful in the sense of being power itself, and He is all-good in the sense of being goodness itself. So the necessary being must be God.

Criticism of the Argument from Contingency

The Universe Might Be Necessary. What does it mean to say, about any X, that X is a contingent being? It means that X might never have existed. How are we to understand this?

One natural explanation is to say that if X is contingent, there was a time in the past when X did not exist. From that point in time, two paths of history stretch forward. On one path, the real path, X exists. On the other path, X does not exist. It is the existence of this other branch of history that allows us to say that X might never have existed. If this is correct, then *for every contingent being, there must be some earlier time at which it did not exist.*

Consider now the whole universe. According to the big bang theory, the universe existed at the very first moment of time. Thus, there is no earlier time at which the universe did not exist, and the universe cannot be a contingent being. It is false that the universe might never have existed; its existence is *necessary.*

Of course, everything *in* the universe is contingent. But it does not follow that if all the *parts* of the universe are contingent, the *whole* universe must be contingent. That would be like saying if each feather in a bag is light, the whole bag must be light. Though everything in the universe is contingent, the whole universe might not be contingent.

Contingent Beings Can Manage by Themselves. The argument from contingency claims that contingent beings depend ultimately on a necessary being. But isn't it possible that contingent beings simply depend *on each other?* Take poor Mr. Jones. His existence depends on his parents' existence, to be sure, and his parents' existence depends on *their* parents, and so on. But why can't we say that Jones's existence is *completely* explained by Jones's parents, and that Jones's parents' existence is *completely* explained by their parents, and so on? Every link in the chain of children and parents is explained by an earlier link. So nothing remains unexplained, and we don't have to call in a necessary being as the explanation of everything.

Defenders of the argument from contingency will say that although each link in the chain is explained, *the whole chain* is not explained: no explanation has been given why there are any parents and children, or why there are any contingent beings at all. But if the existence of *each* contingent being has been explained, shouldn't we say nothing has been left unexplained? Suppose four people are standing on a street corner, waiting for the light to change. One is on his way to lunch, one is on his way to the dentist, one is going for a newspaper, and one is on his way home. We know why each of them is standing on the corner. Do we need some further explanation that tells us why *all four* are standing on the corner together? If we know why each of them is there, we know why all of them are there. Likewise, if we know why each contingent being exists, we know why all contingent beings exist, without ever referring beyond contingent beings.

Goodness Is Not Itself Good.   As we have seen, proving that the necessary being is God takes considerable ingenuity. Thomas Aquinas argued, for example, that the necessary being is the goodness of all good things. It seemed obvious to Aquinas that goodness must itself be good, just as the Greek philosopher Plato (ca. 427–347 B.C.) believed that justice must be just. But this is a mistake. Goodness is a *property of* good things, and it is the things that *have* goodness that are good, *not* goodness itself.

This point can be made in more modern language by talking about *sets,* as we do in the branch of mathematics called set theory. Instead of saying goodness is a property, we can say goodness is *the set of all good things*. Is this set itself good? No. There is no more reason to say the set of all good things is itself good than to say the set of all spoons is itself a spoon.

Fifth Argument for Belief: The Teleological Argument

The cosmological argument and the argument from contingency take as their starting points a common fact: the universe exists. Neither argument makes any reference to the condition of the universe beyond the bare fact of its existence. So far as the first cause argument and the argument from contingency are concerned, the universe could be a pile of Jello, and the argument for God's existence would still go forward. God would be needed to explain the Jello.

By contrast, the teleological argument (from the Greek *telos* meaning goal or purpose) for God takes as its starting point the actual conditions inside the universe. All versions of the argument agree that the universe could not be the way it is unless God acted to make it the way it is.

For Aristotle and the ancient Greeks, the starting point of the teleological argument was the organized pattern of the entire universe, a pattern that could only exist through the action of an intelligent being who organized the universe according to this pattern. For example, the stars and planets keep to their regular patterns in the sky, and on Earth different species of animals breed true: dogs never give birth to cats, and cats never give birth to dogs. In the seventeenth century, Isaac Newton discovered that every bit of matter in the universe obeyed three simple laws of motion and one law of gravitational attraction. If all nature obeyed such laws, philosophers reasoned, there must be a lawgiver, and the supreme lawgiver must be God.

This form of the argument was sharply criticized in the eighteenth century by the Scottish philosopher David Hume (1711–1776). Hume argued that the claim that the *whole* universe has an organized pattern is unfounded, since we can observe only a portion of the whole universe. The pattern we see in our part of the universe might be just a statistical fluke, just as getting five heads in a row when tossing a coin may be due to chance, not to any bias or pattern in the coin. As for Newton's laws, Hume argued that it is a mistake to think of nature as "obeying" these laws. All we know is that so far, nature has *happened* to follow them, but nature is under no compulsion to go on following them. It is quite possible that tomorrow the Law of Gravitational Attraction will be abolished, and objects will fly off the surface of the earth. We do not believe this will happen, but our belief, Hume argued, is not founded on reason. It is just a habit, formed by past experience.

To make the teleological argument work, however, we need not assume the *whole* universe is organized. We need only assume there is *some* organized pattern somewhere in the universe, the existence of which requires supernatural explanation. If we start the argument with this assumption, Hume's objections do not apply. The most discussed example of such an organized pattern is *human life*. Using this example, the teleological argument becomes:

1. Human beings are highly organized bits of matter (Premise 1);

2. Such highly organized bits of matter could only be designed by intelligent action (Premise 2); so,

3. Some intelligent agent designed mankind; but,

4. Only a supremely good and powerful being could design mankind (Premise 3); so,

5. The origin of the human species is God.

There is another bit of organization in the universe that shows divine planning: *the suitability of the earth for human life*. The human race can survive only in a narrow range of physical conditions, and yet these are precisely the conditions we find on earth. Such a correspondence between human beings and their environment cannot be an accident. The correspondence could only result from the actions of an intelligent being who has arranged conditions here to suit the human race.

Premise 2. That human beings are complex organisms (Premise 1) is a plain fact. The teleological argument gets interesting only with the second premise. Does the complexity of human bodies imply pre-existing intelligence?

The forces of nature that we commonly experience seem generally bent on breaking things down. The wind and the waves, diseases and accidents, all contribute to the destruction of life. Complicated things break down into simple things, but simple things never, by themselves, give rise to complicated things. But there is nothing in nature more complicated than the human body and the human brain. Hence, nature by itself could not give rise to human bodies. The human body is made of natural chemicals, but an organizing intelligence was needed to assemble these chemicals into the first human beings.

To suggest this arrangement could occur by chance is ludicrous. As the British philosopher William Paley argued in 1802, the human body is an *artifact,* that is, the product of an artist; and we know an artifact when we see one. Suppose, Paley argued, we are strolling on a sandy beach and come across a metallic object. On one side of the object are numbers and little sticks that keep pace with the movement of the sun, and inside there are many little wheels and springs that keep the sticks moving at the proper rate.

We can ask how this object came into existence. One explanation is that natural forces like the wind and the waves collected little bits of metal and knocked them together into this metallic object, without any consciousness of what they were doing. Another explanation is that an intelligent mind collected the metals and put them together, for the purpose of having an object that will tell the time. No reasonable person would accept the first explanation over the second. The object is obviously a watch, and the existence of a watch implies the existence of an intelligent watchmaker. Likewise, man is a complex object, the parts of which are all arranged to serve the purposes of life and action. Man is an artifact; and if man is an artifact, there must be an intelligent "man-maker."

Premise 3. Call the maker of the human species the Designer of man. Is the Designer of man all-powerful, the source of his own design? If he is not, then we can ask who designed the Designer of man. Since the complex cannot come from the simple, the designer of the designer of man must be more complicated than the designer of man. Who designed this designer? Obviously this question cannot be posed indefinitely; eventually we must come to a Supreme Designer who designed everything else, and who is therefore all-powerful.

What the Supreme Designer does is impose order and pattern on the chaos of nature. But order is better than chaos, and the being that creates order is doing good. Indeed, all goodness is connected to the idea of pattern and the idea of unity in variety. The intelligent organizer of nature is thus the source of whatever is good in nature. The Supreme Designer is supremely good, and since he is supremely powerful as well, it follows that the Supreme Designer must be God.

Criticism of the Teleological Argument

First Objection: The Theory of Evolution. The version of the teleological argument we are considering claims that the complex can *devolve* into the simple, but that the simple cannot *evolve* into the complex. This claim clashes head-on with one of the most famous theories of modern science: the theory of evolution.

Fundamentalist religious leaders see the theory of evolution as the archenemy of religion. That view is false. The theory of evolution is not opposed to all aspects of religion. It is not even opposed to belief in God, and many biologists who accept evolution are devout religious believers. But evolution *is* opposed to the teleological argument, because evolution maintains that the complex *can* evolve from the simple. According to evolution, complex natural phenomena can be produced by natural processes that operate blindly, without any forethought of the objects they produce.

Consider, for example, the argument that *the suitability of the earth for human life shows forethought on the part of a Supreme Designer,* who prearranged the fitness of the earth for life. The evolutionary biologist would say this explanation puts the cart before the horse. Given the environmental conditions on the earth at any time, life-forms that cannot survive under these conditions simply *die off.* The surviving forms are, by definition, compatible with the environment. As the environment changes, life-forms either adapt to these changes or die. So the earth has not been adapted for life; life has adapted to conditions on the earth.

Explaining the existence and organization of human bodies requires a good deal more work. In fact, the original theory of evolution, developed in the nineteenth century by Charles Darwin (1809–1882) and Alfred Wallace (1823–1913), could not fully explain the origin of the human species. But the modern theory of evolution, which added the notion of *mutation* to Darwin and Wallace's concept of *natural selection,* has filled in many of the missing pieces of the story. The story of human evolution, vastly condensed, in the modern theory goes something like this.

Three or four billion years ago, there was no life on earth. Nevertheless, all the chemicals needed for life existed, dissolved in the oceans and in clays under the oceans. These chemicals circulated and were jolted with energy from volcanoes, lightning, and other natural sources. Given millions of years, by chance some of these chemicals were thrown together to form large molecules that had the ability to make replicas of themselves; that is, they had the capacity to reproduce, which is one hallmark of life.

But this process of replication was not perfect, and some of the copies took a different form, some slightly different, some markedly different, from the originals. These new types of living things, called *mutations,* could sometimes make copies of themselves, and their success at replication depended on the suitability of environmental conditions. As environmental conditions changed, the new types sometimes could reproduce better than the older types. The original types were crowded out and died off.

Some of the mutations that occurred were more complicated than their immediate ancestors. On occasion, these more complicated organisms had a better chance of surviving and reproducing than their simpler ancestors. If complexity provides such selective advantages, then we should expect, over time, to find the earth populated by more and more complicated living things. This is exactly what the theory of evolution claims. Life began with single-celled organisms, then proceeded to multi-celled organisms that reproduced asexually, then to multi-celled organisms that reproduced sexually, then to higher animals like the reptiles, then to mammals, and eventually to the human species, which developed from mutations that occurred between 50,000 and 200,000 years ago. The production of the human body is the result of 3 billion years of random shuffling and weeding out: the shuffling of chemical patterns by mutation and the weeding out of species by natural selection. Nothing in the process was pre-ordained; nothing was foreseen by intelligent agents who arranged for it to happen.

The theory of evolution is a scientific theory, and as such, it stands or falls on the evidence. The evidence for the theory of evolution includes *geological evidence,* in which rock strata with early dates frequently contain fossils of less complicated creatures than rock strata of later dates; *biochemical evidence,* including the fact that all animals and plants in the world use a common system of replication based on the chemical labeled DNA; *embryological evidence,* in which embryos of higher animals, including man, develop through a sequence of stages—fish, reptile, and so on—that recapitulate the ladder of evolution; *anatomical evidence,* including vestigial bone structures in higher animals that reproduce the bone patterns of lower animals; and, finally, *laboratory evidence,* in which mutation and selection have been observed in fast-reproducing species like fruit flies.

What about William Paley's watch, lying there on the sand? The evolutionary biologist will say the example is irrelevant. Evolutionary biology explains the development of living things. It says nothing about the creation of dead objects, like watches. The question is not whether natural forces, working for a short while, can produce a watch, but whether natural forces, working for a very long while, could produce a human being.

Despite the evidence, the theory of evolution has numerous critics. One common complaint against the theory of evolution is that the story starts too late, since it starts with the presence on Earth of all the chemicals needed for life. Who arranged for the existence of the right chemicals?

The evolutionist will reply that the chemicals were themselves produced in earlier physical processes, specifically, in the course of giant explosions of stars called *supernovas.* But where did the matter of the supernovas come from? At this point, the evolutionist will say that we are now talking about the origin of matter itself, not the way matter is organized. We have switched from the teleological argument back to the cosmological argument.

There are still, to be sure, missing pieces in the evolutionary story. The mechanism by which nonliving chemicals were brought together into the first self-replicating molecule is not known, and it now seems clear that chance encounters in the primeval ocean are not sufficient to do the trick: the molecules are simply too complicated. It is not known whether the first living things were proteins, which developed DNA as a way to help proteins reproduce, or whether the first living things were DNA molecules, which developed proteins as a way to help DNA reproduce. It is not known whether species slowly evolve into new species or whether there are sudden bursts of evolutionary advance. But there is no reason to think that solving these problems will require giving up the basic ideas of the theory of evolution. The basic notion—that the complex can develop naturally from the simple—has near universal support among scientists.

Second Objection: The Designer Might Not Be God. Suppose that the theory of evolution is wrong and we must postulate an intelligent designer to account for the human species and other patterns in nature. If this designer is not supreme, there must be a designer of this designer. But why must we believe there is one Supreme Designer who designed all the others? Why can't we say each designer has a designer, more complicated than it? For every number, there is another larger number, but it does not follow that there must be one number larger than all the others. Likewise, we can say that each designer has a designer greater than it, but that there need not be one designer greater (and more powerful) than all the rest.

The teleological argument claims that the goodness of the designer is shown by the fact that the basic act of the designer is to impose patterns on chaos. But the imposing of order is not *automatically* good. If it were, the ideal form of government would be military dictatorship. Furthermore, it is not obvious that all goodness and beauty fit the formula of unity in variety. The sky on a cloudless day can be a single beautiful color of blue, and this goodness of color has nothing to do with order or patterns. Without some further development of the theory of value as unity in variety, we cannot claim that the designer of our world is supremely good. As Hume wrote in his *Dialogues Concerning Natural Religion* (1776):

The world, for aught we know . . . is only the work of some infant Deity, who afterwards abandoned it, ashamed of his lame performance; [or] it is the work of some dependent inferior Deity, an object of derision to his superiors. . . .

Sixth Argument for Belief: The Evidence of Miracles

For many religious believers, the main evidence for God's existence lies not in the facts of astronomy or biology but in the events of human history. Events have occurred for which divine intervention is the best—or the only—explanation. Such events are *miracles*.

For Jews, one significant miracle is the deliverance of the Hebrews out of Egypt, which required the parting of the Red Sea. For Christians, the most important miracle is the resurrection of Christ. But there are countless claims of lesser miracles. Indeed, for any person to obtain sainthood in the Catholic faith, two miracles stemming from the intervention of the saint must be authenticated.

For a miracle to prove the existence of God, two conditions must hold. The miracle must have really occurred, and its occurrence could only have been caused by divine intervention. For the Red Sea example, the argument is as follows:

1. The parting of the Red Sea occurred (Premise 1):

2. Divine intervention is the best explanation of the parting of the Red Sea (Premise 2); so,

3. Divine intervention occurred; and

4. This type of divine intervention signifies the existence of God (Premise 3); so,

5. God exists.

The most interesting step in the argument is perhaps Premise 2. Why do believers say that this miracle required divine intervention? Since the days of the Jewish historian Josephus, suggestions have been made to the effect that God did not part the waters. The Jews simply passed through at low tide, and the Egyptians were caught when the tide rushed in.

But *even if* the Egyptians were drowned by the incoming tide, talk about the tides provides no final explanation of what happened. To understand what happened, we must ask why the Hebrews arrived *just* at the moment the tide was out, and the Egyptians arrived *just* at the moment when the tide came in. It looks as if the arrival of the Egyptians and the arrival of the tide were pre-arranged. Indeed, the best explanation of the facts is that they *were* pre-arranged, and that the Hebrews were saved by divine intervention.

Criticism of the Evidence from Miracles

First Objection: Did It Happen? Did the parting of the Red Sea occur? For religious believers, this is a preposterous question, since the event is described in the Bible, which is the revealed word of God, an unimpeachable source. But notice that we are trying here to develop an argument for the existence of God. Until the argument is finished, we cannot rationally assume God exists or rationally assume the Bible is God's word. If we suspend belief in the existence of God, what is the evidence that the miracle occurred?

There is the Biblical record of the event, and that record must be given some weight. On the other hand, it is a little disconcerting that there is no record of this event in any other source; in particular, in any Egyptian source, even though the Egyptians kept records of their military actions. In fact, there is only one (highly disputed) non-Biblical record of the presence of the Hebrews in Egypt at all, and this silence is difficult to reconcile with the Biblical record of the length and size of the Hebrew population in Egypt. And despite the development of underwater archaeology in recent years, no underwater remains of the Egyptian catastrophe have yet been found.

The absence of independent testimony for the miraculous event makes it unreasonable to believe it happened as described. As David Hume pointed out in the eighteenth century, miracles are unusual events that go contrary to what we know about how life works. Thus, the evidence for a miracle must be *stronger* than the evidence for a normal event, because it must overrule not only the contrary evidence that the miracle did not happen, but all our evidence about how life works. The Red Sea miracle, viewed either as an event that violated the physical laws of how water behaves or as a fantastically improbable coincidence, will not meet Hume's standards.

Second Objection: Divine or Natural? Suppose the Red Sea miracle happened. There is still the question of whether the best explanation of the event is natural or divine. The ancient suggestion about the tides is not all that bad. The Egyptian catastrophe could as reasonably be chalked up to bad luck as to divine wrath. The event could have been a coincidence that no one pre-arranged.

How can one rationally distinguish coincidence from pre-arranged events? Suppose an event of type A is followed by an event of type B. Is this a coincidence? Looking at just these two events, it is impossible to tell. But if one observes events of type A invariably followed by events of type B, one might think that events of type A *cause* events of type B and the occurrence of a B after an A is not a coincidence.

If we could observe God and regularly saw God issue commands followed immediately by great natural catastrophes, we might well think the commands of God *caused* the catastrophes. But in fact we do not observe God at all, so we have no evidence for the rule "divine commands cause great catastrophes." Thus, there is no more reason to think the Red Sea story is a miracle than to think it is a coincidence.

Third Objection: The Source of Miracles May Not Be God. *Suppose* the Red Sea miracle occurred and we are satisfied it was not a coincidence. It follows that there is a superhuman source of miracles. The source of miracles may be powerful and good, but the miracles themselves are no proof that the source of the miracle is *all*-powerful and *all*-good. (The Egyptians might think that the source of such miracles is not good at all.)

The source of miracles, though superhuman, might not even be supernatural. When explorers visit tribes deep in the jungle, the actions of the explorers— taking pictures with a Polaroid camera, for example—often look like miracles to the tribespeople. All of the miracles that people have taken as signs of God's power could be the result of interventions on Earth by beings from a civilization more advanced than ours. This, of course, is no proof that such beings exist. But there is no more reason to think miracles are performed by an all-powerful being than there is to think they are performed by *very* powerful but not *all*-powerful beings from outer space.

Arguments Against God's Existence

We have considered six arguments for belief in God and objections to each of those arguments. People who voice these objections obviously reject these six arguments for belief in God. But it does not follow that if they reject these arguments, they must reject belief in God. All they must reject are these six arguments. For all we know, a *seventh* argument for the existence of God *will* work. Rational atheists should not only criticize arguments for belief in God; they should present their own arguments *against* belief in God. We will consider five arguments for atheism.

First Argument Against God's Existence: No Person Is Worthy of Worship

Rachels's Argument About Worship. God is by definition all-good; and from this, Judaism, Christianity, and Islam teach that God is supremely and uniquely worthy of worship. The American philosopher James Rachels, developing some remarks of Kant, has argued that God, so defined, cannot exist. For Kant and for Rachels, *nothing* is worthy of worship: all worship is idolatry, even worship of God. The argument reads:

1.   Something is God only if it is worthy of worship;

2.   Nothing is worthy of worship; so,

3.   Nothing can be God; so,

4.   God does not exist.

Why Nothing Is Worthy of Worship. The Hebrew Bible is full of stories about the wickedness of idolatry: the worship, for example, of idols made of stone. The implied argument is that a mere stone is not worthy of worship, but that Jehovah, the Supreme Being, is worthy of worship. According to Rachels and Kant, however, the problem with worshipping stones is not that stones are unworthy of worship, but that worship degrades human beings. Worshipping requires an attitude of self-abnegation, of saying that one is nothing in comparison with the object of worship. But human beings are not nothing: human beings have reason and freedom of choice, and when they make choices they create their own lives. To worship is to lose self-respect; to worship is to deny the importance of one's own freedom. To do so is to cease to be human, so human beings should never do it.

In particular, a being like God should not be an object of worship. Orthodox worship of God involves a sense of gratitude to God for creating the world and admiration of God for the goodness He has. But to argue that human beings should be grateful to God for creating the world is strange, since creating the world took no effort on God's part, and God's creatures did not ask to be created. And although it is better for God to be good than for God to be evil, one cannot admire God's goodness. God cannot fail to be good. Admiring God for His goodness is like admiring a square for having straight sides.

Criticism of First Argument

First Objection: Worship Consists in Recognizing What God Is and Deserves. When Kant criticized the attitude of worship, he did so objecting to the postures of worship—the bowed head, the bent knee—which in his day were commonly adopted not only in religious services but also in the presence of kings and aristocrats. Kant took these gestures as signifying an attitude that was contrary to human reason. Indeed, it *is* contrary to reason to worship kings and lords: they are just as human as their subjects and vassals. But it is not contrary to reason to worship God. In the case of God, all that worship requires is the recognition of God's power and God's goodness, and these are apprehended by human reason.

Furthermore, God deserves this recognition. True, the creation of the world took no effort on God's part. But in creating the world God created beings with free will, beings whose choices He does not pre-determine. Since human beings are free, God must wait to see what they choose. He must endure their foolish and evil choices, choices that may jeopardize God's whole plan for the universe. The choice to have children always involves the risk of painful rejection by one's own offspring. That God chose to run this risk is worthy of admiration and gratitude.

Second Objection: Worship May Not Be Part of the Essence of God. Judaism, Christianity, and Islam all assume the idea that *God is worthy of worship* follows logically from the idea that *God is all-good.* This assumption makes God's worshipfulness part of the essence of God. But this may be a mistake. There seems to be no contradiction in saying, "God is all-good, but He should not be worshipped." One could accept everything in Rachels's argument and still say, "Yes, nothing is worthy of worship—but an all-powerful and all-good being nevertheless exists."

Second Argument Against God's Existence: No Person Can Be Omnipotent

According to Thomas Aquinas, there are many things God can't do. He can't make a round square; He can't make two plus two equal five; He can't change the past; He can't create a married bachelor. Does this show that God is not omnipotent? Not at all. An omnipotent being can do everything that can be done. But these are logically impossible acts. They simply cannot be done.

Some atheists have argued, however, that there is at least one *logically possible* action no one, not even God, can do. Consider a stone too heavy for anyone to lift. Either God cannot make this stone or God can. If God cannot make the stone, then there is something He cannot do—make the stone. If God can make the stone, then there is something that He cannot do—lift the stone. Either way, there is one thing that God cannot do. It follows that there can be no such thing as an omnipotent being. And from this it follows that there cannot be a God.

Criticism of the Second Argument

Some theists have suggested that the solution to the puzzle is that God cannot make the stone because such a stone is logically impossible. *A stone too heavy for an omnipotent being to lift* is like *a round square*; and, as Aquinas argued, an omnipotent being is not required to be able to make one.

But the atheist is not likely to find this answer convincing. This solution assumes that such stones are inconsistent with the existence of omnipotence, and the existence of omnipotence is the very thing that we are arguing about. Suppose I say, "Psychic powers do not exist, because no one can predict what the stock market will do tomorrow." It would not be fair to reply, "A stock market that a *true* psychic could not predict is logically impossible." It is the existence of true psychics that we are arguing about.

Perhaps a better solution is to say that God *could* make this stone, but He *chooses* not to. An all-powerful being is one that has the *ability* to do all possible things, but He need not *actually* do all possible things. In fact, God has good reasons not to make this stone. The moment He made such a stone, He would cease to be omnipotent because He could not lift it. At that moment, He would cease to be God.

Third Argument for Atheism: No Person Can Be Both Omniscient and Omnipotent

Because God is omnipotent, God is not subject to the flow of time. On the contrary, according to theologians God exists outside of time, in the sense that every moment is equally present to God. Thus, God perceives future events as if they were happening now, and knows from eternity what the future course of events will be. Now if God knows the future perfectly, He knows His own future decisions. It follows that God cannot change His mind about anything.

But the God of the Hebrew Bible is depicted as having free will and changing His mind. For example, after Jonah announces that God has commanded that Nineveh be destroyed in forty days, the king and people of Nineveh repent:

And God saw their works, that they repented of their evil way: and God repented of the evil, that he said that He would do unto them, and He did it not. (Jonah 3:10)

Likewise God changed his mind when Abraham pleaded for the people of Sodom (Genesis 18) and when Moses pleaded for the children of Israel (Exodus 32). An omnipotent being should be able to make changes like these.

If God sees his future decisions as if they are present, He could no more change his mind about a future decision than He could change his mind about a past decision. Thus, either God is not free, or He does not know His future decisions. Either He is not omnipotent, or He is not omniscient.

Three Responses from Theists

Theists have proposed at least three ways of resolving this conflict between omnipotence and omniscience. Some suggest that God's omnipotence should be restricted to allow for His omniscience. Others suggest that God's omniscience must be restricted to allow for His omnipotence. Still others think that omnipotence and omniscience can be reconciled without any restrictions at all.

Orthodox Protestants assert that God foresees all events and that all events are therefore predetermined. It follows that God cannot change the course of future events, nor can He change any of His decisions. In one sense, this limits God's power. But in another sense, it exhibits God's omnipotence, since it shows that all events flow from a divine plan that is so perfect it never needs to be changed.

More radical theists assert that God does have the power to change His mind. On this view, God does not know all of His future decisions. In one sense, this limits God's omniscience. But in another sense, God is still omniscient. He still knows everything that can be known. God's future decisions simply cannot be known by anyone, not even by God.

Catholic thinkers generally follow Aquinas and try to have it both ways. They assert that God foresees all future events. But they also agree with the radicals that God can change his mind about things. Thus, when God changes His mind, He foresees that He will change his mind. His foreknowledge does not deprive Him of His freedom of will, since there is a difference between foreseeing an event and forcing it to happen.

The three responses of theism disagree with each other. They cannot all be true. But if any one of them is true, the paradox of omniscience and omnipotence is resolved.

Fourth Argument for Atheism: No Person Can Be Perfectly Good

God, by definition, is perfectly good. It follows that He must be perfectly just and perfectly merciful, since justice and mercy are two varieties of goodness. But how can anyone be perfectly just and perfectly merciful at the same time? A perfectly just person will give each wrongdoer exactly the punishment he or she deserves. A perfectly merciful person will give wrongdoers less than the punishment they deserve. Thus, it is strictly impossible for anyone to be perfectly just and merciful.

The Theists' Reply

Most theists agree that God gives everyone exactly what he or she deserves. But they also claim that God is perfectly merciful. Divine mercy does not imply that God gives wrongdoers less than they deserve. What divine mercy implies is that God gives everyone the power and the opportunity to obtain salvation.

God's mercy, then, is different from human mercy. Human mercy acts *after* a just sentence is pronounced. God's mercy acts *before* the final judgment. But when the final judgment arrives, there will no more forgiveness.

Fifth Argument for Atheism: The Problem of Evil

The atheist's best-known argument has been saved for last:

1. God is perfectly good;

2. A perfectly good being should want to destroy all evil;

3. God is all-powerful;

4. An all-powerful being can destroy any evil; therefore,

5. If God exists, there will be no evil; but,

6. Evil exists; so,

7. God does not exist.

Though most religious believers recognize that the existence of evil poses a difficult problem for theism, few realize how difficult a problem it is. If God is all-good and all-powerful, then any world He creates must have *no* imperfections; it must be, as Leibniz said, the best of all possible worlds. If there is a single blot on the world's perfection, a single drop of unnecessary evil, then there is no God. One cannot evade this conclusion by pointing to all the good things in the world: the problem is that there are evil things as well. One cannot evade this problem by producing explanations of *some* or *most* of the evil in the world: the theist must explain every last drop of it. Furthermore, whatever explanation the theist produces must be more plausible than the atheist's blunt and simple explanation of the world's evil: evil exists because there is no God to prevent it.

Since the theist must explain all the world's evil, it is fair for the atheist to ask for an explanation of one form of evil that is particularly troubling and tragic: the suffering of small children. In the world, many children suffer pain, disease, starvation, and early death. Certainly a perfectly good being would *want* to relieve their suffering, and an all-powerful being *could* relieve it. Yet they suffer, and the reason they suffer is that there is no God to save them.

Weaknesses in Traditional Solutions to the Problem of Evil

An honest, unflinching look at the suffering of children shows that many traditional solutions of the problem of evil are quite weak.

The Original Sin Solution. The Bible implies that the evils in the world result from the original sin of Adam and Eve (Genesis 3:16–17). We are all children of Adam and Eve, so we all share in their moral weakness. No one is innocent; no one deserves happiness. Since no one deserves to be happy, no injustice is done if anyone suffers, even if the suffering person happens to be a child.

The original sin solution assumes that children are not innocent since they share in a moral weakness, a potential for sin, that afflicts the whole human race. But it hardly seems fair to punish children because they have the *potential* to sin. It is only fair to punish people for crimes that they *do* commit, not crimes that they *might* commit. Children are innocent in the simple sense that they have not *yet* done anything wrong, whatever their moral weaknesses might be.

Even if we agreed that all human beings are guilty simply because they are human beings, we still must explain why some people suffer *more* than others. If the amount of original sin in each person is the same, the punishment should be the same. Since some people suffer more than others, at least some of the world's evil is unexplained by reference to original sin.

The Devil Solution. A second solution suggested in the Bible is that the evils of the world result from the actions of superhuman evil beings, or devils, directed by the devil Satan. For example, it is Satan who inflicted sufferings upon Job, a perfect and upright man in the land of Uz (Job 1:12).

Why should God choose to create Satan and let him loose in the world? If God exists, this is the best possible universe. In the best possible universe, one would expect every grade of being to exist, from the most primitive to the most advanced. Thus, in the universe there must be intelligent creatures more powerful than human beings. Furthermore, since freedom is good, God has endowed these superhuman creatures with the freedom to choose between good and evil. As it happens, at least one of these creatures, Satan, chose evil, but God could not prevent Satan's choice without depriving Satan of free will, a gift He had already irrevocably bestowed. Thus, Satan is responsible for the evil of his choices, and God is responsible only for the good of Satan's freedom.

But even if we accept the existence of devils, this does not fully solve the problem of evil, for we must explain why a good God would let devils torture children. God must give the devils free will, but the devils will have free will if they are allowed to torture each other; their freedom does not require that they torture human children. It is a mistake to suggest free will requires the freedom to do everything, including torturing children. If that were true, then human beings would lack free will simply because they cannot fly.

The Heavenly Rewards Solution. Among Christians, it is widely believed that the suffering of the innocent on earth is compensated by rewards in heaven. Suffering during life is counterbalanced by eternal bliss after death, an eternal bliss that is guaranteed to all children who suffer and die: "Blessed are the poor in spirit, for theirs is the kingdom of heaven. . . . Blessed are the pure in heart, for they shall see God (Matthew 5:3, 8)."

The heavenly rewards solution implies that it is always morally permissible to allow children to suffer if this suffering makes them better off later. This is implausible. Suppose a sadistic billionaire kidnaps and tortures a child for about two hours. He then releases the child and anonymously establishes a trust fund for $1 million in the child's name. Even if we think that, on balance, the child is better off after the torture than before, we would hardly think the billionaire's action is just. It seems similarly difficult to think God would be just, even if He set aside great rewards in heaven for the children He permits to suffer on earth.

The Evil as Privation Solution. Developing some remarks of Aristotle, Thomas Aquinas argued that the theist is not required to explain the evils in the world, because, strictly speaking, these evils do not exist. Evil, Aquinas argued, has no reality of its own: evil is a *privation* of good.

A privation is a kind of absence of reality, a shadow of a real thing. Consider, for example, the hole in a doughnut. The hole has no reality of its own; it is simply the place where the dough is not—a "privation" of dough. If the doughnut is good, then the hole in the doughnut is an absence of good. Likewise, Aquinas argued, everything real in the universe is good, and the places where evil exists are just privations of this good. Evil does not exist in its own right, no more than the hole in the doughnut can exist without the doughnut.

One problem with Aquinas's solution is that it seems very implausible when applied to one of the prime evils of the universe, the evil of pain. Pain is nothing more, and nothing less, than an unpleasant feeling. Consequently, if a person truly feels a pain, the pain truly exists. Admittedly, the pain may result from a privation of health, but the pain itself is real, not a privation of anything.

Furthermore, Aquinas provides no argument why we should think that evil is a privation of good, rather than thinking that good is a privation of evil. Aquinas assumed the universe was fundamentally good, because he believed the universe was created by a good God. Since it is the existence of a good God that is questioned by the atheist, this assumption cannot be used to prove the universe is basically good. If we suspend belief in God, is it any more reasonable to think the universe is basically good, with evil spots, than to think it is basically evil, with good spots?

The Evil as Contrast Solution. In the fifth century A.D., St. Augustine argued that a world with some evil in it is better than a world in which there is no evil. A world without evil is a world without contrasts and without interest; a world with evil is an exciting world in which people are provided with a meaningful task: the task of defeating evil, or at least enduring it bravely. In a related argument, Leibniz suggested that evil must exist or else it would not be possible for people to *appreciate* the good things in life.

These arguments from Augustine and Leibniz do explain *some* of the evil in the world. But they fall far short of explaining the pain of every suffering child. Perhaps for contrast and variety, we need some evil in the world. But does the world need *so much* suffering in order to be interesting? Does the world need *so much* suffering before people appreciate the difference between evil and good? If one fewer child died of cancer each year, would the world be any less interesting or would the human race appreciate the good any less?

In 1949, British author C. S. Lewis attempted to defend theism and answer these questions by arguing that the idea that there is *so much* evil in the world contained a deep philosophical mistake. Lewis admitted the world contained many evils. But Lewis thought it was a mistake to think these evils could be *added together,* like quantities of a liquid, so that we could make a rational judgment about the quantity of evil in the universe. If we each have a headache, two evils exist, but the two headaches cannot be added together to form a single sum of evil bigger than the original. After all, there is no single mind in which those two headaches fuse into a kind of Superheadache. But, if we cannot add evils together, we cannot conclude there is too much evil in the universe. All we need to explain, then, is why there is *any* evil in the universe at all, and this is accomplished by the evil as contrast solution.

But the problem of the suffering of children concerns not just the *quantity* of their suffering but also its *justice.* Is it morally right to ask children, let us say, *two-year-old* children, to endure bravely the suffering and death that cancer and other diseases inflict on them? Is it fair that *some* should suffer in order that *others* have an interesting world to live in? Is it fair that *some* should suffer in order that *others* might appreciate how good it is to live without suffering? No, says the atheist, it is not fair; *life* is not fair, so it is implausible, almost ridiculous, to suggest that the world is governed by a good God.

The Reincarnation Solution to the Problem of Evil

Most discussions of the problem of evil and the suffering of children assume that the children who suffer are innocent. Since the innocent do not deserve to suffer, the fact that God permits their suffering to go on seems unjust.

But suppose children in the world today have lived many former lives, that in fact they are reincarnations of people who lived in the past. If this is true, then the sufferings of children in the present world may be just punishments for sins committed in former lives. The suffering of children, therefore, far from being a proof of divine injustice, may be a proof of divine justice, which guarantees that every wicked person will receive what he or she deserves, either in this life or the next.

The idea that present suffering is invariably punishment for past sins is not widely accepted in the West, but hundreds of millions of Hindus accept it, calling it the truth of *karma*. From the standpoint of pure logic, reincarnation provides perhaps the most direct and most satisfactory reconciliation between the goodness of God and the suffering of children. But this explanation will succeed only if the doctrine of reincarnation is true. That is one of the topics debated in Part II.

SUGGESTIONS FOR FURTHER READING*

The Judeo-Christian-Islamic Conception of God

For a comparison between the concept of deity presented here and alternative concepts of absolute beings, see Charles Hartshorne and William L. Reese, eds., *Philosophers Speak About God* (Chicago: University of Chicago Press, 1953); H. P. Owen, *Concepts of Deity* (New York: Herder and Herder, 1971); and J. N. Findlay, "Why Christians Should Be Platonists," in D. J. O'Meara, ed., *Neoplatonism and Christian Thought* (Albany: SUNY Press, 1982).

The most majestic survey of the properties of God in Christianity is Thomas Aquinas, *Summa Theologica**, Book I, A. Pegis, trans. (New York: Random House, 1945). Aquinas discusses the goodness of God in Question 6 and the power of God in Question 25. For a contemporary study of the concept of God, see James Collins, *God in Modern Philosophy* (Chicago: Regnery, 1959) and R. G. Swinburne, *The Coherence of Theism* (Oxford: Oxford University Press, 1977).

For an analysis of God's power, see Harry Frankfurt, "The Logic of Omnipotence,"* *Philosophical Review* (1964); for God's knowledge, see A. N. Prior, "The Formalities of Omniscience,"* *Philosophy* (1962); for God's eternity, see Nelson Pike, *God and Timelessness* (New York: Schocken Books, 1970), and Paul Helm, *Eternal God* (New York: Oxford University Press, 1989).

The Question of Existence

One good study of the meaning of the claim "God exists" is James F. Ross, *Philosophical Theology* (Indianapolis, Ind.: Hackett, 1980, Ch. 3).

Contemporary philosophy has spent much time on the question of what it means for something to exist. For general surveys, see Milton Munitz, *Existence*

---

* These listings include references to books and to articles published in philosophy journals. Back issues of journals are available in most university libraries. An asterisk after a title indicates an advanced technical discussion.

*and Logic** (New York: New York University Press, 1974), and C. J. F. Williams, *What Is Existence?** (Oxford: Oxford University Press, 1981). The most influential modern discussion is "On What There Is,"* in W. V. O. Quine, *From a Logical Point of View* (Cambridge, Mass.: Harvard University Press, 1953).

Why the Existence of God Is Important
One of the most moving accounts of the psychological relevance of belief in God is found in Blaise Pascal's seventeenth-century description of "the misery of man without God," in *Pensees,* W. F. Trotter, trans. (New York: Modern Library, 1941, Ch. 2). See also Bertrand Russell, "A Free Man's Worship," in Paul Edwards, ed., *Why I am Not a Christian* (New York: Scribner's, 1957).

Believing "on Faith"
For an argument that proofs of God's existence are beside the point, see Steven Cahn, "The Irrelevance to Religion of Philosophical Proofs of the Existence of God," *American Philosophical Quarterly* (1969). Important discussions of the view that religious belief needs no rational foundation include the essays by Norman Malcom and Colin Lyas in Stuart Brown, ed., *Reason and Religion* (Ithaca, N.Y.: Cornell University Press, 1975).

For discussions of the relation between faith and reason, see Thomas Aquinas, *Summa Contra Gentiles,** A. Pegis et al., trans., (Garden City, N.Y.: Doubleday, 1956); John Hick, *Faith and Reason* (Ithaca, N.Y.: Cornell University Press, 1957); Basil Mitchell, *The Justification of Religious Belief* (New York: Seabury, 1973); and R. G. Swinburne, *Faith and Reason* (New York: Oxford University Press, 1984).

First Argument for Belief: Pascal's Wager
The argument was stated by Pascal in *Pensees,* Ch. 3.

Criticism of Pascal's Wager
For modern studies of the logic of the argument, see James Cargile, "Pascal's Wager," *Philosophy* (1966); Ian Hacking, "The Logic of Pascal's Wager,"* *American Philosophical Quarterly* (1972); Terence Penelhum, *God and Scepticism* (Boston: Reidel, 1973); Michael Martin, "On Four Critiques of Pascal's Wager," *Sophia* (1975); Anthony Flew, *God, Freedom, and Immortality* (Buffalo: Prometheus Press, 1984); and Nicholas Rescher, *Pascal's Wager* (Notre Dame, Ind.: University of Notre Dame Press, 1985).

Pascal's Wager Revised
The revised version of Pascal's Wager amounts to what is called the pragmatic argument for belief in God. A classic statement is William James, "The Will to Believe," in *The Will to Believe and Other Essays in Popular Philosophy* [1896]; for discussion, see W. I. Matson, *The Existence of God* (Ithaca, N. Y.: Cornell University Press, 1964, Part IV), and Richard Gale, "William James and the Ethics of Belief," *American Philosophical Quarterly* (1980).

Criticism of the Revised Wager

The criticism of the revised version of Pascal's Wager assumes that happiness is a state of knowledge, not just a state of feeling. For studies of the relationship between emotion and knowledge, see Robert Solomon, *The Passions* (Garden City, N.Y.: Doubleday, 1976), and Robert M. Gordon, *The Structure of Emotions* (Cambridge: Cambridge University Press, 1987). The Dream Machine question is discussed by Robert Nozick, *Anarchy, State, and Utopia* (New York: Basic Books, 1974).

A famous and very different criticism of pragmatic religious belief is W. K. Clifford, "The Ethics of Belief," in W. K. Clifford, ed., *Lectures and Essays* (London: 1879).

Second Argument for Belief: The Ontological Argument

Anselm's original version of the ontological argument is in his *Proslogion,* M. J. Charlesworth, trans. (Notre Dame, Ind.: Notre Dame University Press, 1979, Chs. 2–4). Descartes's version is found in the fifth of his *Meditations,* John Cottingham, trans. (New York: Cambridge University Press, 1986).

The ontological argument was defended by Spinoza in his *Ethics** [1676], I, Propositions 7–11, and by Leibniz in his *New Essays Concerning Human Understanding.* [1710] IV, Ch. 10 and Appendix x.

A nice collection of modern essays discussing the ontological argument is *The Ontological Argument,* Alvin Plantinga, ed. (New York: Doubleday, 1965). The most eloquent defender of the ontological argument in contemporary philosophy is Charles Hartshorne, *The Logic of Perfection* (La Salle, Ill.: Open Court, 1962), and *Anselm's Discovery* (LaSalle, Ill.: Open Court, 1965). Readers of Hartshorne's books will note that he concentrates on the modal form of the argument ("God is a necessary being"; therefore, "God exists"), which is not discussed here.

Criticism of the Ontological Argument

Gaunilo's criticisms are included in Charlesworth's translation of Anselm's *Proslogion,* cited above.

Kant's criticisms of the ontological argument were published in 1781 in his *Critique of Pure Reason: Transcendental Dialectic,** ii, Ch. 3, Sect. iv (1781), Norman Kemp Smith, trans. (New York: St. Martin's Press, 1933).

Interpreting Kant's views on existence is difficult. He seems to hold that existence is the link that holds the properties of a thing together. For exegesis, see Alex Orenstein, *Existence and the Particular Quantifier** (Philadelphia: Temple University Press, 1978, Appendix).

Russell's argument why there are no nonexistent things is stated in "On Denoting,"* in R. G. Marsh, ed., *Logic and Knowledge* (London: Allen and Unwin, 1956). Russell's analysis of existence was turned against the ontological argument by J. N. Findlay in "Can God's Existence Be Disproved?" [1948], reprinted in Findlay's *Language, Mind, and Value* (London: Allen and Unwin, 1963).

Third Argument for Belief: The Cosmological Argument

Aquinas defends the cosmological argument in his *Summa Theologica** I, Question 2, Article 3. Some modern studies are W. L. Rowe, *The Cosmological Argument* (Princeton, N.J.; Princeton University Press, 1975), and Richard Swinburne, *The Existence of God* (Oxford: Oxford University Press, 1979, Ch. 7).

Premise 1. One nice exposition of Big Bang theory is James Trefil, *The Moment of Creation* (New York: Collier, 1983). Some of the relationships between Big Bang cosmology and the cosmological argument for God are discussed in Paul Davies, *God and the New Physics* (New York: Simon and Schuster, 1983).

Stephen Hawking, *A Brief History of Time* (New York: Bantam Books, 1988), introduces some speculations that would, if proven, undercut his earlier proof that the beginning of the cosmos is a singular point of infinite density. In the new account, time "wraps around" the Big Bang. Accordingly, the Big Bang is no more the beginning of time than the North Pole is the beginning of the earth.

Premise 2. Leibniz's discussion of the idea that "nothing is simpler and easier than something" is in his essay, "On the Ultimate Origin of Things" [1697], reprinted in Philip P. Weiner, ed., *Leibniz Selections* (New York: Scribner's, 1951). A related argument was given in 1704 by Samuel Clarke, *A Demonstration of the Being and Attributes of God,* discussed in Rowe's *The Cosmological Argument.*

Kant's discussion of universal causation is "Second Analogy," in his *Critique of Pure Reason**. The reader should note that though Kant believed every event in time has a cause, he did not himself think that law could be used to prove the universe was caused by God. Every cause, for Kant, must be a possible object of experience, and God is not an object of experience.

Premise 3. Few authors have attempted to demonstrate that the creator of the universe must be God. One who does is Stanley Jaki, *Cosmos and Creator* (Chicago: Regnery, 1980, Ch. 2).

Criticism of the Cosmological Argument

The Universe Might Have Begun Spontaneously. A simple historical introduction to quantum physics still worth reading is Banesh Hoffmann, *The Strange Story of the Quantum* [1942] (New York: Dover Publications, 1959). The problem of causality is probed in David Bohm, *Causality and Chance in Modern Physics* (New York: Harper's, 1961). Three new popular expositions are Gerald Feinberg, *What Is the World Made Of?* (Garden City, N.Y.: Doubleday, 1978); Paul Davies, *Other Worlds* (New York: Simon and Schuster, 1980); and Nick Herbert, *Quantum Reality* (Garden City, N.Y.: Doubleday, 1985). The argument that the universe might be a quantum fluctuation is discussed in Heinz Pagels, *Perfect Symmetry* (New York: Doubleday, 1985).

The Creator Might Not Be God. For a survey of possibilities that different cultures have explored concerning the relationship between the creator and the universe, see Milton Munitz, *Space, Time, and Creation* (New York: Dover Publications, 1981, Ch. 1).

Fourth Argument for Belief: The Argument from Contingency

The argument from contingency, called "the argument from possibility and necessity," is given by Aquinas in *Summa Theologica**, Question 2, Article 3. A modern discussion in these terms is Bruce Reichenbach, *The Cosmological Argument* (Springfield, Ill.: Charles Thomas, 1972).

Interesting discussions of the concept of a necessary being include John Hick, "Necessary Being," in John Donnelly, ed. *Logical Analysis and Contemporary Theism* (New York: Fordham University Press, 1972); Alvin Plantinga, "God and Necessity," in *The Nature of Necessity* (Oxford: Oxford University Press, 1974); and R. L. Swinburne, "Kinds of Necessity," in *The Coherence of Theism,* Ch. 13.

Criticism of the Argument from Contingency

The argument that contingent things can fully explain the existence of other contingent things is made by Bertrand Russell, "The Existence of God: A Debate," in Paul Edwards and Arthur Pap, eds., *A Modern Introduction to Philosophy* (Glencoe, Ill.: Free Press, 1973). See also, Paul Edwards, "The Cosmological Argument," *The Rationalist Annual* (1959), and Anthony Kenny, *The Five Ways* (London: Routledge and Kegan Paul, 1969).

Fifth Argument for Belief: The Teleological Argument

Aquinas develops the teleological argument with reference to the order of the universe in *Summa Theologica* I, Question 23, Article 3. One classic exposition that focuses on the existence of life is William Paley, *Natural Theology* (Indianapolis, Ind.: Bobbs-Merrill, 1963). Modern defenses of the teleological argument are Richard Taylor, *Metaphysics* (Englewood Cliffs, N.J.: Prentice-Hall, 1963); Donald Mackay, *Science, Chance, and Providence* (Oxford: Oxford University Press, 1978); and Robert Hambourger, "The Argument from Design," in Cora Diamond and Jenny Teichman, eds., *Intention and Intentionality: Essays in Honor of G. E. M. Anscombe* (Ithaca, N.Y.: Cornell University Press, 1979).

Criticism of the Teleological Argument

David Hume's criticisms of early versions of the teleological argument are given in his *Dialogues of Natural Religion* [1779], Part 9. A modern Humean critique is D. H. Mellor, "God and Probability,"* *Religious Studies* (1969).

First Objection: The Theory of Evolution. Darwin's views are mainly in two books, *The Origin of Species* [1859] and *The Descent of Man* [1871], issued together as a Modern Library Giant (New York: Random House, n.d.). A helpful summary is Benjamin Farrington, *What Darwin Really Said* (New York: Simon and Schuster, 1966). A classic attack on the teleological argument from the standpoint of evolution is Clarence Darrow, *The Story of My Life* (New York: Scribner's, 1932, Ch. 4).

For the modern theory of evolution, see G. G. Simpson, *The Meaning of Evolution* (New Haven, Conn.: Yale University Press, 1949); Jacques Monod, *Chance and Necessity* (London: Collins, 1972); and Richard Dawkins, *The Blind Watchmaker* (New York: Norton, 1986). For the specific problem of the origins of life on Earth, see Robert Schapiro, *Origins* (New York: Summit Books, 1986).

It is possible that the natural mechanism by which the complex evolves from the simple involves not just chance mutation and natural selection but also the spontaneous organization of a system driven far from equilibrium by external forces. See Ilya Prigogine and Isobelle Stengers, *Order out of Chaos* (London: Heineman, 1984).

Religious believers who deny evolution and maintain the simultaneous creation of species are called creationists. Creationism is defended in Henry Morris, *Scientific Creationism* (San Diego, Calif: Creation-Life, 1974), and attacked in Michael Ruse, *Darwinism Defended* (London: Addison-Wesley, 1982), and Philip Kitcher, *Abusing Science* (Cambridge, Mass.: MIT Press, 1983).

Second Objection: The Designer Might Not Be God. For Hume's argument that the creator might not be God, see *Dialogues Concerning Natural Religion,* Part V.

Sixth Argument for Belief: The Evidence of Miracles

A good starting point for the study of miracles is R. G. Swinburne, *The Concept of Miracle* (London: Macmillan, 1971). The idea that miracles could provide evidence for the existence of God is defended by George Schlesinger, *Religion and Scientific Method* (Dordrecht: Reidel, 1977, Ch. 22). See also, Robert Hambourger, "Belief in Miracles and Hume's Essay," *Nous* (1980).

Criticism of the Evidence from Miracles

The most famous critical analysis of the evidence from miracles is David Hume, "Of Miracles," reprinted in *An Inquiry Concerning Human Understanding* (Indianapolis, Ind.: Bobbs-Merrill, 1955, Section X). For analysis, see Leslie Stephen, *English Thought in the 18th Century* Vol 1, 3rd ed. (London: 1902), and C. D. Broad, "Hume's Theory of the Credibility of Miracles," *Proceedings of the Aristotelian Society* (1916–1917).

Arguments Against God's Existence

For defenses of the atheist outlook, see Richard Robinson, *An Atheist's Values* (Oxford: Oxford University Press, 1964), and Anthony Flew, *The Presupposition of Atheism* (New York: Harper and Row, 1976). Two famous twentieth-century atheist philosophers are Bertrand Russell and Jean Paul Sartre. See Russell's *Why I Am Not a Christian* (New York: Scribner's, 1957), which oscillates between atheism and agnosticism, and Sartre's *Being and Nothingness,* Hazel Barnes, trans. (New York: Philosophical Library, 1956).

First Argument Against God's Existence: No Person Is Worthy of Worship

Worship is analyzed in Ninian Smart, *The Concept of Worship* (London: Macmillan, 1972). Rachels's argument was published in *Religious Studies* (1971) and reprinted in Paul Helm, ed., *Divine Commands and Morality* (Oxford: Clarendon Press, 1977).

Criticism of First Argument

Rachels's argument is attacked in Philip Quinn, *Divine Commands and Moral Requirements* (Oxford: Oxford University Press, 1978).

Second Argument Against God's Existence: No Person Can Be Omnipotent

A forceful statement of the problem of the-stone-too-heavy-for-God-to-lift is J. L. Cowan, "The Paradox of Omniscience,"* *Analysis* (1965).

Criticism of the Second Argument

Various attempts to solve the puzzle of the stone are G. B. Keene, "A Simpler Solution to the Paradox of Omnipotence," *Mind* (1960); Barnard Mayo, "Mr. Keene on Omnipotence,"* *Mind* (1961); George Mavrodes, "Some Puzzles Concerning Omnipotence," *Philosophical Review* (1963); and C. Wade Savage, "The Paradox of the Stone,"* *Philosophical Review* (1967). For other solutions, see L. Urban and D. Walton, eds., *The Power of God* (Oxford: Oxford University Press, 1978).

Note that the suggestion that God could create the stone but would then cease to be God is incompatible with the popular theistic view that God's existence is necessary and that he *cannot* fail to exist.

Third Argument for Atheism: No Person Can Be Both Omniscient and Omnipotent

For the relation between God's knowledge and events in time, see Norman Kretzmann, "Omniscience and Immutability," *Journal of Philosophy* (1966), and H. N. Castaneda, "Omniscience and Indexical Reference,"* *Journal of Philosophy* (1967). For other arguments about the logical incompatibility of omniscience and omnipotence, see John Fischer, "Freedom and Foreknowledge," *Philosophical Review* (1983), and Steven Brams, *Superior Beings* (New York: Springer-Verlag, 1983, Ch. 4).

Three Responses from Theists

The view that God knows future events and that free will does not exist therefore pre-determined is developed in Jonathan Edwards, Paul Ramsey, ed., *Freedom of the Will* (New Haven, Conn.: Yale University Press, 1957).

The view that God cannot know future contingent events is associated with Rabbi Levi ben Gershon (1288–1344) and is restated in Douglas Lackey, "A New Disproof of the Compatibility of Foreknowledge and Free Choice,"* *Religious Studies* (1974). The implications of placing God *within* time are assessed in the modern school of thought called "process theology." See John C. Cobb, *Process Theology* (Philadelphia: Westminster, 1971).

That God knows future contingents but that this does not entail determinism is argued by Aquinas in *Summa Theologica* I, Question 14, Article 13. A modern defense of this position is Alvin Plantinga, *God, Freedom, and Evil* (New York: Harper and Row, 1974, pp. 69–72). For criticism, see Philip Quinn, "Plantinga on Foreknowledge and Freedom,"* in James Tomberlin and Peter Van Inwagen, eds., *Alvin Plantinga* (Boston: Reidel, 1985).

Fourth Argument for Atheism: No Person Can be Perfectly Good
The problem that different kinds of goodness are incompatible with each other is poignantly developed by Isaiah Berlin, "On the Pursuit of the Ideal," *New York Review of Books* (March 17, 1988): 35–44.

The Theist's Reply
Aquinas addresses the problem of reconciling justice and mercy in *Summa Theologica** I, Question 21, Article 4.

Fifth Argument for Atheism: The Problem of Evil
Statements of the problem of evil that leave it an unsolved challenge to theistic belief include David Hume, *Dialogues Concerning Natural Religion* X and XI; John Stuart Mill, "Nature," in *Three Essays on Religion* [1874]; J. L. Mackie, "God and Omnipotence," *Mind* (April 1955); Anthony Flew, "Divine Omnipotence and Human Freedom," *New Essays in Philosophical Theology* (1955); and H. J. McCloskey, "God and Evil," *Philosophical Quarterly* (April 1960). The arguments of Mackie and Flew are combatted by Ninian Smart, "Omnipotence, Evil and Supermen," *Philosophy* (April 1961).

Weaknesses in Traditional Solutions to the Problem of Evil

The Original Sin Solution. For the doctrine of original sin, see Jonathan Edwards, C. H. Holbrook, ed., *Original Sin* (New Haven, Conn.: Yale University Press, 1970).

The Devil Solution. The adequacy of the devil solution is defended in Alvin Plantinga, *God, Freedom, and Evil* (New York: Harper and Row, 1974).

The Heavenly Rewards Solution. For the concept of heaven, see Bas van Tersel and Edward Schillebeeckx, eds., *Heaven* (New York: Seabury, 1979). One very sophisticated use of the heavenly rewards solution is developed by J. N. Findlay, *The Transcendence of the Cave* (London: Allen and Unwin, 1967, pp. 170–171).

The Evil as Privation Solution. Aquinas takes up the problem of evil in *Summa Theologica** I, Questions 47–49.

The Evil as Contrast Solution. St. Augustine discusses the problem of the world's evil in his *Confessions* VII, Chs. 3–5 and *The City of God,* Book XI, Chs. 16–18. For analysis, see G. R. Evans, *Augustine on Evil* (New York: Cambridge University Press, 1982). Leibniz's discussion stretches through his *Theodicy* [1710], E. M. Hubbard, trans. (Indianapolis, Ind.: Bobbs-Merrill, abridged ed., 1966).

Richard Swinburne, *The Existence of God,* Ch. 11, agrees that none of the aforementioned solutions succeeds in explaining why there is *so much* evil in the world.

The argument that evils cannot be summed together was developed by C. S. Lewis, *The Problem of Pain* [1949] (New York: Macmillan, 1962), and revived by John Taurek, "Should the Numbers Count?"* *Philosophy and Public Affairs* (1977). For criticism, see Derek Parfit, "Innumerate Ethics,"* *Philosophy and Public Affairs* (1978).

For other solutions to the problem of evil, see Josiah Royce, *Studies in Good and Evil* [1888] (Hamden, Conn.: Archon, 1964); John Hick, *Evil and the God of Love* (New York: Harper and Row, 1978); Harold S. Kushner, *When Bad Things Happen to Good People* (New York: Schocken Books, 1981); Abigail Rosenthal, *A Good Look at Evil* (Philadelphia: Temple University Press, 1987); and Robert Merrihew Adams, *The Virtue of Faith** (New York: Oxford University Press, 1987).

For further criticisms of solutions to the problem of evil, see J. L. Mackie, *The Miracle of Theism* (Oxford: Clarendon Press, 1982).

The Reincarnation Solution to the Problem of Evil

A nice introduction to reincarnation in a variety of religions and contexts is Joseph Head, ed., *Reincarnation* (New York: Warner Books, 1978). For the Hindu doctrine of karma, see Geoffrey Parrinder, *The Indestructible Soul* (London: Allen and Unwin, 1973), and Ninian Smart, *Doctrine and Argument in Indian Philosophy* (London: Allen and Unwin, 1964, Ch. 12).

PART II

The Possibility of Life After Death

The Concept of Life After Death

The question of whether there is a life after death troubles philosophers and ordinary people alike. Most people hope death is not the end of life, but rather the beginning of a new stage of life. They hope their own consciousness will not be snuffed out by death, and pray they will some day be reunited with friends and loved ones from whom they have been separated by death. As we saw in Part I, ideas about life after death are also intimately connected with thoughts about the justice of the universe. If there is a life after death, then in the next life good people may receive the just rewards they have so far been denied, and evil people may receive the just punishments they have so far evaded. Furthermore, the reincarnation theory of life after death provides a fairly effective solution to the problem of reconciling the evils of this present life with the goodness of God. But does life after death, in *any* form, exist?

Before considering arguments, we must first define terms. To begin, we need a definition of "death," and we need a definition that does not prejudge the question of whether there is a life after death. A definition of death such as "the separation of the soul from the body," for example, is of no use for our purposes, since this definition already assumes people have souls that somehow survive death. Likewise, a definition of death such as "the destruction of the personal self" is of no use, since this definition already implies that there is *no* life after death. We will define death as "the cessation of biological life in the brain"; that is, we will take "death" to mean "brain death." Although not very precise, this definition at least does not prejudge the question of whether there is a life after death.

Next, we need to specify more carefully what we mean by "life" when we talk about "life after death." One point on which most people agree is that it makes no sense to talk about a person's life after death unless that person is *aware of things* after death. Life after death without consciousness is not a human life at all. A meaningful human life after death requires basic mental activities, like thinking, understanding, and remembering. It does not seem to require much more. It would be nice, in a life after death, to be able to engage in physical activities like walking and running; to be able to see, hear, and have sense perceptions; and to communicate with other people. But none of these activities is strictly necessary in order to have a life after death. So we will equate "being alive after death" with "thinking after death."

There is one further factor essential to survival after death: the *personal identity* factor. If a human being, (call him "Jones") is to have a life after death, Jones, not somebody else, must exist after death. When I hope for life after death, I hope *I* will survive; that is, that the very person who I now am will survive death.

Of course, after death, I will be different from the way I am now. But I am different now from the way I was when I was three years old, and I still have the same *personal identity*. If I say, "First I lived in Queens, but now I live in New Jersey," the pronoun "I" refers to a *single* person at two different points in time. Similarly, if I have a life after death, I must be able to think, "I used to live in America, but now I'm someplace else," where, once again, the pronoun "I" refers to a single person at two different times.

By what rules do we refer to the *same* person at *two* different points in time? Philosophers call such rules "the criteria of personal identity." Understanding and applying the criteria of personal identity are not just issues for philosophers. Every day, in law courts, juries and judges struggle with problems of personal identity. Is the accused, now standing in the courtroom, the same person as the person who committed the murder? Should Daisy, who claims to be Daddy Warbucks's long-lost daughter, receive the money assigned to Warbucks's daughter in his will?

If we think about these problems we realize that all of us use two different criteria of personal identity, depending on the problem at hand. One criterion is a *physical* criterion: we judge that *A is the same person as B if A has the same body as B.* For example, if the murderer has the same fingerprints as the accused, we infer that the murderer has the same body as the accused; from this we conclude the murderer is the same person as the accused. The other criterion is a *psychological* criterion: we judge that *A is the same person as B if A knows things only B could know.* If Daddy Warbucks told his daughter a secret and Daisy convincingly reveals the secret in court, most juries will award the inheritance to Daisy.

Many philosophers will object that the jury in the Daddy Warbucks case might have acted hastily. After all, Daddy Warbucks's real daughter could have revealed the secret to Daisy, who is not the daughter but only an impostor. Strictly speaking, what are the "things only B could know"? It seems the only thing that B, and nobody but B, could know is *what it has been like to have B's experiences*. If we combine this fact with the psychological standard, we get this rule of personal identity: *A is the same person as B if A remembers experiences had by B.*

We will call this rule the Memory Criterion. I can know I am the same person as a certain boy who attended grammar school in Queens if I can remember that boy's experiences of the first day at school: what the teacher looked like, what her voice sounded like, and so forth, from the perspective of that boy sitting in the classroom.

In Part II, we will consider two common views about life after death. One is the view that, at death, a person's body dies but his or her consciousness (or soul) lives on, without a body. This is the *pure soul* theory of life after death. The other is the view that, at death, the body dies but the person lives on in a different body. This is the *reincarnation* theory of life after death.[1]

According to both the pure soul theory and the reincarnation theory, a person does not have the same body after death as before death. It follows that the physical criterion of personal identity cannot be used, for either theory, to establish life after death. Only the Memory Criterion will do. In short, we say that Jones has a life after death if

1. Jones suffers brain death at *t*; and

2. There is some person after *t* who remembers experiences had by Jones.

Must We Die Before We Know?

Many people believe we cannot know, while we live, whether there is a life after death; but after we die, we will know for sure. This view is curious. If I die and there is *no* life after death, then I will not "know for sure" that there is no life after death, since I will not know anything at all.

On the other hand, if there *is* a life after death, perhaps we can know about it without experiencing it. The principle that we can know things only if we experience them, or receive reports from others who have experienced them, is simply too strict. We know the center of the sun is hot, even though no one has ever gone to the center of the sun. Likewise, we might be able to know, on the basis of circumstantial evidence, that there is a life after death, without any help from direct experience or eyewitness testimony.

Furthermore, why should we assume that we have *no* eyewitness testimony

---

[1] The Christian doctrine of life after death, which claims that the disembodied soul survives death and then is reunited with a resurrected body at the Last Judgment, combines the pure soul and reincarnation theories and needs no separate consideration.

concerning life after death? Reports about life after death are at least as old as Homer's *Odyssey,* in which the great traveler Odysseus visits the underworld and converses with the ghost of Achilles. Let us consider one type of "eyewitness" report as our first argument for the reality of life after death.

First Argument for Life After Death: Near-Death Experiences

In the early 1970s, the American author Raymond Moody made headlines by describing the experiences of persons who were very close to death. These people reported that, during the period when they were dead or nearly dead, they had the experience of being separated from their bodies and floating through space, usually down a dark tunnel and toward a bright light, around which they caught glimpses of long-dead relatives.

If these experiences really occurred, some explanation of them must be given. For Professor Moody, the explanation is simple: these people were having perceptions of the next world, in which people live on after finishing their stay in this one.

Moody and other chroniclers of such near-death experiences are of course aware that sceptics will dismiss such experiences as hallucinations. But if these experiences are hallucinations, why are they so similar to each other? If one person says that he or she saw a flying saucer on Main Street, but no one else saw it, the rest of us will conclude that he or she was dreaming or lying. But *twenty-five* people, each reporting independently that they saw a flying saucer on Main Street, provide strong evidence that their experiences were not hallucinations. The rational conclusion is that these experiences were perceptions of a flying saucer that was really there. Likewise, if dozens of people report experiences of a bright light in a tunnel not in this world, the simplest explanation is that they really saw the light.

Criticism of Reports of Near-Death Experiences

Sceptics insist, nevertheless, that these reports are not perceptions of the next world, that better explanations of near-death experiences are possible.

The experiences might be hallucinations. True, the hallucinations are similar to each other, but it is possible for many people to have similar hallucinations. If we take a poll of 1,000 people, perhaps twenty will report that, last night, they dreamed they were falling. These twenty experiences of falling are similar to each other, but the similarity does not prove these people actually fell during the night. Moody and other collectors of near-death experiences do not report how many near-death experiences they collected and what percentage of these reports mentioned the dark tunnel, the bright light, and the faces of dead relatives. Perhaps only a small percentage of people near death have these experiences, in which case the similarity of the experiences proves nothing.

Alternatively, these near-death experiences might be perceptions—jumbled perceptions—of *this* world. People who are near death are not likely to be thinking clearly, or understanding correctly what is going on around them. The dark tunnel might be nothing more than the hospital corridor through which they were wheeled on their way to the emergency room. The bright light might be a ceiling bulb, or a penlight shone in the person's eyes to check the contraction reflex of the pupils. People near death misinterpret these experiences as perceptions of the next world, perhaps because they believe they have already gone there.

Finally, even if these people *were* perceiving another world, their experiences provide no proof that it is possible to live there. These persons were near death—some were even "declared" dead—but Moody and similar authors do not mention any case in which the persons involved were provably dead. A proof of life after death requires experiences *after* death, not *near* death. We need proof, not of another universe, but of another life.

Second Argument for Life After Death: Memories of Former Lives

Although the major Western religions do not maintain the doctrine of reincarnation, a surprising number of people in the West and billions of people in Asia believe they will continue to live on in new and different bodies when their present bodies are destroyed. Is there evidence to back up this common belief?

Many people feel that they possess personal evidence of reincarnation. For example, almost everyone has experienced déjà vu, the strange feeling that "I was in this place before, but I've never been here before." Some people are convinced they have previously seen certain places they never visited before in this life. From this they conclude they must have visited these places in a former life. Viewers of the movie *Patton* will recall the scene in which General Patton walked about the ruins of ancient Carthage, remarking that he was sure he had lived there, 2,000 years ago.

In addition to the near-universal experience of déjà vu, some individuals claim to remember detailed experiences from their former lives. In the middle 1950s, for example, a woman in Colorado named Veronica Tighe claimed, under hypnosis, to remember in great detail experiences she had while living in early nineteenth-century Ireland in the body of a woman called Bridey Murphy. Tighe's claim caused a national sensation; and many people, listening to tape recordings in which Tighe recounted her nineteenth-century experiences, felt that the coherence and detailed character of the Bridey Murphy stories proved the stories were true. Many cases similar to the Bridey Murphy case have been reported. If just *one* of these reports is true, then reincarnation exists in some form.

Criticism of Alleged Memories of Former Lives

If in fact a person has visited a place before, but not in this life, the doctrine of reincarnation is proven. But sceptics argue that feelings of déjà vu provide no proof a person actually visited a place in some former life. Déjà vu is just a feeling, and feelings can be inappropriate or mistaken. People on occasion have felt they could fly and have died jumping off buildings. Likewise, people can feel, in all sincerity, they have previously visited a place, when in fact they never visited the place at all.

Some explanation must be given for déjà vu, but good explanations of déjà vu need not involve reincarnation. Perhaps the person experiencing déjà vu visited a place in the past that *resembles* the place that causes déjà vu. If so, the uncanny feeling of déjà vu is not caused by mystical memories of the *same* place, but by confused memories of some *similar* place, the precise details of which have been forgotten with time.

In the Bridey Murphy case, questions were raised from the start about the credibility of Veronica Tighe's story. Despite intense detective efforts in Ireland, no trace of a Bridey Murphy fitting Tighe's descriptions was ever found. Was Tighe remembering the experiences of Bridey Murphy, or was she making up the Bridey Murphy story, piece-by-piece? (This is not to say that Tighe was lying: she could have sincerely believed something that she only imagined was really true.) The coherence and complexity of the Bridey tapes, which impressed many listeners, prove nothing. In his novel *Anna Karenina,* Leo Tolstoy told a coherent and detailed story about the lives of 155 different people, and none of these 155 people ever existed as described except in Tolstoy's mind.

Stories of reincarnation vary and the criticism given here of the Bridey Murphy reports may not apply to other cases. Nevertheless, there is a systematic criticism that can be made of *all* reports that allege reincarnation. Whenever a person says that he or she remembers an event from some past life, either (1) we cannot verify the past event occurred, or (2) we can verify the past event occurred. If we cannot verify that the past event occurred, then we have no right to believe it happened. But if we can verify, by some method, that the past event really occurred, then the person who claims reincarnation may have learned about the past event *using the same method we did.* If so, there is no more reason to believe a person is reincarnated because he or she knows about the past event than there is reason to believe *we* are reincarnated because we know about the past event.

Suppose a man claims he is a reincarnation of Napoleon, and he remembers the battle of Waterloo. If he gives details of the battle that historians cannot check, then we have no reason to believe they happened. If he gives details known to historians, then for all we know he got these details from a book about Waterloo.

Third Argument for Life After Death: Communication with the Dead

Perhaps the simplest proof for the existence of life after death would be to produce evidence of communication with the dead. Communication requires mental processes; and if a dead person succeeds in communicating with us, then life after death exists.

There are numerous reports of communication with the dead. Communication, some claim, can even take place in a controlled fashion, during seances, in which a medium establishes contact with the spirit of a dead person, who communicates through the medium's mouth. The events at some seances have been so impressive that many distinguished scientists and philosophers, like the British philosopher C. D. Broad, have become convinced that communication with the dead has occurred. What has especially impressed observers is the ability of some mediums to present reports in the language of the dead person, when this language is not known to the medium herself or himself. Since no person can speak a language unless she or he knows the language, the medium, in these cases, must be under the control of a person who does know the language—presumably the spirit of the dead person. There are so many of these reports that it is highly unlikely all of them are false.

Criticism of Reports of Communication with the Dead

We will not consider here any concrete examples of seances or other communications with the spirits of the dead. Though many mediums have been exposed as frauds, those who trust in seances will simply assert that some *other* medium is authentic. The only way to criticize faith in seances is to present a general argument showing how difficult it is to establish that communication with the dead has occurred.

When a medium claims to have contacted a dead person, it is reasonable to demand proof that the contact is real and not just the invention of the medium. A thoughtful Mr. Jones will insist that the medium present some secret fact, known only to the dead person and himself, as proof that the contact is real. But a *very* thoughtful Mr. Jones will realize that, even if the medium produces the secret, this is still no proof communication with the dead has occurred. There is one other source from which the medium might obtain the secret. That source is sitting, full of life, right at the seance: it is Jones himself! Even if he is confident the secret has not slipped out during a conversation with the medium, even if he is confident the medium has not obtained the secret from him by hypnosis, Jones must acknowledge that the medium might have obtained it from him by mental telepathy.

Those who have faith in seances cannot avoid this criticism by scoffing at the idea of mental telepathy, since it is only by telepathy (mind-to-mind contact) that communication with dead persons can proceed. Spirits have no tongues and cannot whisper into the ear of the medium. A denial of the existence of telepathy would lead to the conclusion that communication with spirits is impossible.

This leaves those fascinating cases in which mediums "speak" a language they claim never to have learned. In such cases, it is fair to ask whether the medium is really communicating in the language, or merely parroting word sounds in the language. To speak a language is to be able to hold a conversation in it. Usually when the medium speaks a new language, no conversation in the language is occurring: the medium speaks and the people in the audience listen. Furthermore, even if the medium did succeed in holding a conversation in a language she or he did not know, this might prove she or he is possessed by a spirit that knows the language, not by the spirit of a *dead person*. It might be, to use a religious example, merely some devil playing a trick on the world.

What evidence, then, would really show that communication with the dead has occurred? Perhaps the following would do. At a seance, the medium claims to be possessed by the spirit of a dead sea captain whose ship sank in the seventeenth century. The medium reveals the location of the ship (not previously known), and divers retrieve a casket from this ship. Archaeologists verify that the casket has not been opened for 300 years. When the casket is opened, it contains the ship's log, just as the medium predicted. So far, this is not proof, since the medium could have discovered this with X-ray vision. But it turns out the log is written in code, and none of the world's cryptographers can make sense of it. The medium, however, succeeds in cracking the code, which turns out to have been written in a randomized personal cipher only the sea captain could have known.

Nothing like this has ever happened, but if it did, it would be a pretty good proof that communication with the dead had occurred. Or would it?

Some Further Problems in Proofs of Immortality

The preceding sections have given criticisms of evidence presented to show that human beings survive death. Suppose these criticisms are no good, and some story of reincarnation memories or spirit contact is true. The sceptic will point out that one such true story cannot show that human beings survive death.

The true story proves *one* person has survived death, but this does not prove *all* people survive death. Perhaps some people survive death while others do not, just as some people survive cancer while others do not.

Furthermore, because one person survives death, we should not think this person will live *forever*. Possibly human beings survive their present death only to cease to exist at some later date. After their present death, their consciousness or souls might live on for a while and then slowly evaporate; or, after death, they might be reincarnated once, and then never reincarnated again. But when people say they hope they will survive death, what they really hope for is everlasting life. None of the previous arguments comes close to proving *that*.

Fourth Argument for Life After Death: God Will Provide

For many religious believers, belief in life after death is grounded in belief in God. It would be cruel if good people perished; but God is not cruel, so good people do not perish.

For most such people, God reveals his intentions in Scripture. In the Hebrew Bible, God says almost nothing about life after death. But for Christians, the promise is clear: "He that believeth in Me shall have everlasting life" (John 6:47).

Criticism: Even the Good Do Not Deserve Salvation

Obviously the fourth argument for life after death is sound only if God exists. Since the existence of God was the subject of Part I, we will not take it up again. Let us now simply assume God exists. Would this, by itself, guarantee life after death?

The argument given here claims that good people *deserve* everlasting life, so a good God will provide it to them. But certainly it cannot be argued that God *owes* good people anything. Since God, if God exists, has been the principal benefactor of the human race, it can hardly be true that God is now in debt to the human race. On the contrary, the human race is in debt to Him. When a good person says he deserves something from God, he is, in fact, saying, "I owe you everything: so you must give me more!"

In the Gospel according to St. John, Christ promises eternal life to those who follow Him. But the gospels never say that those who follow Christ *deserve* to be saved. The gospels say only that those who follow Christ *will* be saved. Consequently, life after death for good people cannot be deduced from the justice of God. One could learn that Christ is "the resurrection and the life," not from reason, but from revelation alone.

First Argument Against Life After Death: Evolution Implies Mortality

The human race is a part of nature, not something apart from nature. Human beings are products of mutation and natural selection—biological descendants of primitive apes, reptiles, amphibians, fish, and one-celled organisms that drifted through the primordial sea. The marks of this evolutionary process are stamped on the early stages of every human life, which starts out as a one-celled organism, develops into a jellyfish-like colony, develops a body with gills and the head of a tadpole, grows a mammalian body with bones for a tail, and only later assumes something like human form in its mother's womb. If we deny life after death to protozoa, fish, amphibians, reptiles, and apes, how unreasonable it is to award life after death to human beings, the evolutionary children of protozoa, fish, amphibians, reptiles, and apes! To say that lower animals die but human beings live forever creates a gap between human beings and lower animals that the whole thrust of evolutionary theory rejects.

Furthermore, there is no reason to assume the evolutionary process has reached its pinnacle. The sun has burned for only half its lifetime; perhaps the evolutionary process on this planet is only half finished. And besides the sun, there are 100 billion stars in the local galaxy and 100 billion galaxies in the universe. Given these numbers, it is highly likely there are other inhabited planets, and very unlikely, out of all the inhabited planets, that the human species is the most developed form of life. Perhaps species exist who would find the suggestion that human beings live forever as comical as human beings find the suggestion that frogs live forever. Given the likelihood of forms of life *higher* than human beings, isn't it strange to think that the dividing line between species with immortal souls and species without souls should come exactly between human beings and chimpanzees?

Criticism: Thought Is More Fundamental Than Any Physical Process

The theory of evolution claims that everything about human beings, including their thoughts, is the result of physical processes. But how do we know the theory of evolution is true? How do we know any theory is true? We develop theories because our experiences present us with puzzles, and our theories help us solve these puzzles. Evolution, the Big Bang, atomic particles, and so forth, are just concepts we use to organize and make sense of our experiences. That our experiences exist we can know for sure; what they are like we can know for sure. But that the theory of evolution is true, or that Big Bang cosmology is true, is only a matter of conjecture. Thus, our experiences, which are essentially mental—or spiritual—are more fundamental, more real, than any physical process.

How odd it would be if concepts like evolution and the Big Bang, which are constructions of the human mind, could turn on their creator and prove that human minds must die! That would be like one of the characters in a novel standing up and shooting the author dead at his desk.

As for the suggestion that the universe teems with species more advanced than man, no single piece of real evidence for their existence has ever been found. People often ask: If the aliens are so advanced, why haven't they contacted us? The truth is that the human species is fundamentally different from any other known animal. So far as we know, only this planet has life; and, on this planet, only the human species has *language*.

Second Argument Against Life After Death: Consciousness Depends on Brain Processes

Thoughts and other states of consciousness are fairly mysterious, and philosophers have not been able to agree on their nature. But even if we do not know the nature of consciousness, we can know that consciousness depends for existence on brain processes. It follows that if brain processes stop with death, consciousness must stop as well.

That consciousness depends on brain processes can be seen from considering what we know from the study of electroencephalograms (EEGs), which measure electrical activity in the brain. EEGs are usually employed to detect abnormal brain activity, but they can be used to study normal activity as well. Psychologists and neurologists who use EEGs can judge from a sample electroencephalogram whether a person is conscious or unconscious, or whether he or she is in a state of light or deep sleep. Obviously, a lower level of brain activity is associated with deep sleep than with light sleep. These facts about EEG levels provide the following argument against life after death.

If U is the EEG level below which a person is in deep sleep, then

1. EEG levels less than U are correlated with deep sleep;

2. After death, a person's EEG is permanently at zero; so,

3. After death, a person is at best in a deep sleep; but,

4. In deep sleep, a person has no perceptions or thoughts;

5. To have a life after death, a person must be capable of perceiving or thinking; so

6. There is no life after death.

Step 2 of this argument states established scientific fact. Steps 1 and 5 are true by definition. The key point in the argument, then, is step 4, which states that when a person is in deep sleep he or she perceives nothing: his or her mind, in short, is a complete void, without memories or dreams. But how can we know that persons in deep sleep have blank minds?

The answer is that *observation* and *personal reports* provide the evidence that justifies step 4. Whenever we observe persons in deep sleep, with an EEG level less than U, we observe that their eyes are closed, their body relaxed, and they do not have the jerky eye motions that usually accompany dreams. Furthermore, persons who have been below level U themselves assert that their minds were blank during deep sleep. They report that they can remember nothing, not even dreams, that happened to them during the time they were in deep sleep. Thus, we have a perfect correlation between deep sleep and *reports of* blank minds. From this, we should infer that deep sleep is, in fact, correlated with a blank mind.

Criticism: A Report About Deep Sleep May Be Mistaken

Those who believe in life after death will argue that this story about EEGs provides no decisive evidence of mind/brain dependence. The argument claims the correlation between low EEG readings and *reports of* blank minds shows that low EEG readings indicate an absence of consciousness. But the demonstration fails because the reports could simply be mistaken.

If we observe people in deep sleep, it seems that their minds are blank, because they are perfectly motionless, their eyes don't jerk around, and so forth. But this appearance might be deceptive: internal states do not necessarily manifest themselves in external behavior. Just as mathematicians, when they concentrate on a difficult problem, might seem to be in a stupor, though their minds are very active, so also a person in a deep sleep might seem to have a blank mind, while in fact his mind is active and full of thoughts.

The argument that people cannot *remember* any experience they had during deep sleep is also unconvincing. Because a person cannot remember an experience is no proof that he or she never had it. That I cannot remember the experiences I had between 12 noon and 12:05 P.M. one year ago is no proof my mind was blank for those five minutes. That I cannot remember the experiences of my first birthday is no proof I had no experiences on my first birthday. Likewise, a person may have all kinds of experiences during deep sleep and yet not remember them upon awakening. Thus, even if we admit death is like a permanent deep sleep, we can argue that, during sleep and death, the mind continues to have experiences.

Third Argument Against Life After Death: Thoughts Are Themselves Physical (The Thesis of Materialism)

The second argument against life after death claims that consciousness depends on brain processes. The third and final argument against life after death goes one step further. It does not merely say that consciousness *depends on* brain processes. It says that consciousness *is* a brain process. Ordinarily, we think the mental and the physical are two different things. But according to this new argument, the mental is *not* different from the physical. On the contrary, mental things are a subclass of physical things.

The thesis that the mental is a subclass of the physical is called *materialism.* (Some philosophers prefer the term *physicalism.*) Materialists believe human beings are just living bodies, nothing more, and human minds are identical with living human brains.[2] In particular, materialists deny that human beings possess

---

[2] More precisely, this is the materialism philosophers call central state materialism. The other varieties are not considered here, but all types imply that there is no life after death.

souls, if by a "soul" one means a nonphysical entity not made of atoms but capable of consciousness.

If materialism is true, when a person's body is destroyed all mental activities of that person cease. Thus, if materialism is true, a person cannot exist as a pure consciousness without a body. Furthermore, if materialism is true, reincarnation is unlikely. According to materialism, a person's memories are simply states of his or her brain. When the brain dies, all memories disappear. After Jones dies no person will remember Jones's experiences, so no person after Jones dies will be a provable reincarnation of Jones.

The theory of materialism has ramifications that go far beyond the question of life after death. Some philosophers maintain that if human beings are purely physical, then all human actions are subject to physical laws, and what people call "free will" does not exist. Others believe that if human beings do not have souls, then someday human beings can be surpassed and supplanted by advanced computers. Furthermore, the thesis of materialism is an essential part of Marxism, which is the official philosophy of one-quarter of the world's population. If materialism is false, then Marxism is false. Obviously, much rides on whether or not materialism is true.

First Argument for Materialism:
Mind-Brain Correlations

It does not take any special scientific or philosophical knowledge to realize there is a close connection between the mind and the brain. If we hit a person hard enough on the head, that person will lose consciousness. The blow to the head creates a condition in the brain, and the related unconsciousness is a condition of the mind. The repeated association between head blows and states of unconsciousness constitutes a *mind-brain correlation*.

There are many mind-brain correlations. The presence of certain drugs in the brain will almost invariably be correlated with hallucinations in the mind. Other drugs are correlated with the alleviation of pain. Brain specialists have created fairly detailed maps of brain sectors, indicating which parts of the brain are related to various mental processes. There is a given location in the brain associated with speech, another associated with memory, another with visual perception, and so on. There is every reason to hope that, as investigation continues, these maps will be improved, and the rules relating brain sectors to mental functions will become more and more specific. Recently, for example, scientists have discovered that a few simple nerves (neurons) in the brain are responsible for perceiving the orientation and intensity of light. Ultimately, it should be possible to determine, based on a careful scan of Jones's brain, that Jones is thinking now of his dear Aunt Tillie.

Since there are so many correlations between the mind and the brain, the materialist argues that we should conclude that mental events are identical with brain events. The materialist feels confident in drawing this conclusion because we frequently draw similar conclusions in our everyday lives. Suppose we hear that someone robbed a bank in Manhattan last Friday night. The bank robber was observed to have red hair, blue eyes, a slight limp in his left leg, and a tattoo of an eagle on his right forearm. Then suppose we notice that our new next-door neighbor has red hair, blue eyes, a slight limp in his left leg, and a tattoo of an eagle on his right forearm. We might think the bank robber and our next-door neighbor must be the same person. The number of correlations between the bank robber and our neighbor is too great to be a coincidence. Likewise, the materialist argues that the number of correlations between the mind and the brain is too great to be a coincidence. The correlations exist because the mind and the brain are simply the same thing.

Criticism: Correlations Do Not Prove Identity

For anti-materialists, the idea that a correlation between things of type A and things of type B proves that things of type A *are identical with* things of type B is simply false. Suppose we inspect a glove factory that has produced a million pairs of gloves. For every right-hand glove there is a left-hand glove, and vice versa. Furthermore, there are no features a right-hand glove has that a left-hand glove lacks, and no features a left-hand glove has that a right-hand glove lacks. If one is velvet, so is the other, and so forth. The right-hand gloves are perfectly correlated with the left-hand gloves. But we should *not* conclude from this that right is identical with left, or that any right-hand glove is identical with a left-hand glove. But if we should not say, given right-left correlations, that right equals left, we should not say, on the basis of mind-brain correlations, that mind equals brain, or that mental events are brain events.

Second Argument for Materialism: Interaction Between Mind and Body

Critics of materialism say that the mind is not identical with the brain or any other physical thing: in short, the mind is a nonphysical *soul*. But if the human mind and the human body are so different in nature, how is it possible for the mind and the body to interact with each other?

That the mind and body do interact is something nobody can deny. Suppose, for example, a student decides to ask a question and subsequently raises her hand. This process begins with something mental—the thought of asking a question—and ends with something physical—the motion of the student's hand. Or suppose a person puts his hand on a hot stove and feels pain caused by the heat. This process begins with something physical—the hand on the stove—and ends with something mental—the consciousness of pain. Each person undergoes thousands of such mind-body interactions every day.

For the materialist, all these mind-body interactions are physical and can be fully explained by physical science. The thought in the student's mind is an event in the brain, which is connected to the hand motion by physical nerves and muscles. The consciousness of pain caused by heat is an event in the brain, which is connected by nerves with the burnt skin surface. There is no mystery how information gets from the hand to the mind in either case: it goes through the nerves.

Now suppose the mind is not material, but spiritual—a soul. How can a decision in the soul produce a motion in the hand? How can heat applied to a hand produce pain in the soul? If the connection between soul and body is spiritual, it cannot get attached to the body; and if the connection between soul and body is physical, it cannot get attached to the soul. The soul does not exist in physical space: it cannot be affected by physical energy, and it cannot supply physical energy to the body. How then can it affect or be affected by the body? The materialist claims that these questions cannot be answered and, because these questions cannot be answered, souls do not exist.

Criticism: Interaction Does Not Require Contact

The materialist argues that interaction between the soul and the body is a mystery because there can be no contact between the soul and the body. The hidden assumption in this argument is that A cannot influence B unless A is in contact with B. But this assumption is false even in the physical realm. The moon influences the earth and causes the tides, but the moon is not, in any obvious way, in contact with the earth. Just as there is no point of contact at which the moon influences the earth, there is no point of contact between the soul and the body. Yet the moon does influence the earth, and the soul does influence the body. Influence and connection can be two different things.

To say that the soul can influence the body is to say that a cause in the soul can have an effect in the body. Does the relationship of cause and effect require that the cause be in contact with the effect? The philosopher David Hume, who developed the most penetrating analysis of the nature of causes and effects in the history of philosophy, denied that causes must be connected with their effects. According to Hume, when we say *an event of type A is the cause of an event of type B,* all we can justifiably mean is that *we have observed events of type B follow events of type A with such regularity that we have come to expect, when we observe an A, it will be followed by a B.*

If Hume is right about the nature of causation, then there is no difficulty in the idea that an event in the soul can be a cause of an event in the brain. All that is required is that events of type A in the soul have been observed to be regularly followed by events of type B in the brain. For example, if the thought "I will now raise my hand" is regularly followed by my hand rising, then I am entitled to say my thought was the cause of the motion of my hand. That my thought is non-physical and my hand is physical is no bar to the existence of cause and effect relations between souls and hands. Thus, materialism cannot claim it is the only theory that can explain interactions between the mind and the body.

We turn now to arguments *against* materialism. We will consider seven very different arguments, so different that they cannot *all* be true. But all seven arguments point to the same general conclusion: that people are more than just bodies, even living bodies; that, indeed, they have souls.

First Argument Against Materialism: Thoughts Lack Physical Properties

Materialists maintain that thoughts are physical entities. But physical entities have physical properties that thoughts simply do not have.

All physical objects have shape and mass. States of consciousness have no shape or mass. (What shape does a stomachache have?) Physical objects can be seen and touched; states of consciousness cannot be seen or touched. Every physical object has a definite location, but some mental events have no definite location. (If a person says he feels a pain in his leg, after his leg has been amputated, the pain cannot be in his leg, since he has no leg.) Physical objects obey the laws of physics: an object in motion remains in motion unless affected by an external force. Do thoughts in motion remain in motion?

Furthermore, states of consciousness have psychological qualities that no physical thing seems to have. Suppose a person feels a throbbing, piercing toothache. We can examine her teeth as much as we want, but we will not find a tooth that is throbbing or piercing. (Teeth throb and pulsate only in cartoons.)

Thus, thoughts lack physical properties, and body parts lack psychological qualities. From such facts many people and some philosophers have concluded that mental states *cannot* be physical and physical states cannot be mental. Materialism is false.

The Materialist Replies: Thoughts Are Events, Not Objects

The materialist believes the first argument against materialism is based on confusion about what materialism really maintains. The materialist *agrees* that thoughts do not have shape or mass, cannot be touched, and so forth. This indeed shows that thoughts are not physical *objects*. But according to materialists there are *two* kinds of physical entities: physical *objects* and physical *events*. Physical objects, automobiles for example, have shape and mass. Physical events, automobile *accidents* for example, occur at a certain place and time, but have no shape or mass. Automobiles can be touched, but automobile accidents cannot be touched. *Thoughts should be classified as events:* they are more like automobile accidents than like automobiles. That they have no shape or mass does not prevent them from being physical.

A thought is, to be sure, a special kind of physical event. It has certain causes and it produces certain effects. The causes of thoughts are events in the body's nervous system, and the effects of thoughts are a person's behavior. But the thought itself is an event in the brain. We can no more have thoughts without brain cells than we can have automobile accidents without automobiles. If this is so, the puzzle about the location of the pain in an amputated leg is solved. The pain is located, not in the amputated leg, but in the amputee's brain.

What about the throbbing, piercing toothache? The toothache, says the materialist, is a brain event. If we examine this brain event, we will not find any property of the event itself that is its "throbbingness" or "piercingness," because the agony of the pain is not a property of pain itself but a relation *between* the pain and its *effects*. If we look at a pain by itself, we cannot tell if it is agonizing, just as we cannot tell if a man is a father by looking at him. We can only tell that a man is a father if we see his children, and we can only tell that a pain is agonizing if we see the person writhing and groaning, or at least wincing a little.

Second Argument Against Materialism: Descartes and Doubt

Descartes developed our second argument against materialism. He reasoned that if there were a single feature the mind possesses but the brain does not, then the mind and the brain must be different things. The special feature Descartes believed the mind possessed but the brain did not was *certainty of existence*. Descartes argued:

1. I cannot be certain I have a body;

2. I can be certain I have a mind; so,

3. The mind has a feature (certainty of existence) that the brain does not have; but,

4. If X has a feature that Y lacks, X ≠ Y; so,

5. The mind is not identical with the brain.

Step 1 asserts that we cannot be certain we have bodies. In fact, Descartes went even further: he maintained we cannot be certain the physical universe exists. The reason is that our only evidence for the existence of our brains, or our bodies, or the physical universe, is the evidence of our senses: what we can see and what we can touch. We can be deceived, however, by such sense perceptions. When we dream, we think we see and touch things, and they are not really there. If *each* sense perception could be an illusion, then *all* sense perceptions could be illusions. Our lives might be just one long dream from which we will awake someday. It might be that I do not have a body, but only dream that I have one. Perhaps I am a pure spirit, deceived by the Devil into thinking I have a body.

These are fantastic thoughts, but they are not impossible thoughts. Since they describe possibilities, they cast some doubt, a slight doubt, on my opinion that I possess a body. But if a slight doubt exists, then I cannot be absolutely certain I have a body.

Descartes' argument that I can be certain I have a mind (step 2) is equally ingenious. He pointed out that doubting is a mental process; consequently, nobody can justifiably doubt he or she has a mind. One needs a mind in order to be able to doubt; thus, any doubt about the existence of one's mind would be self-refuting. Another way of putting this is to say that since believing is a mental process, every person's belief that he or she has a mind must be true, and every person's belief that he or she lacks a mind must be false. It follows that I can be absolutely certain I have a mind.

Notice that Descartes is not saying persons should believe that they have no bodies. All he is saying is, if we think about it, we cannot be sure we have bodies; and if we think about it, we can be sure we have minds. Think about it!

The Materialist Replies: Certainty About X Is Not a Feature of X

Suppose Descartes is right that (1) I can be certain I have a mind, but (2) I cannot be certain I have a body. Does it follow, as Descartes claims in step 3, that the mind has some feature the body lacks? Suppose I am at the racetrack and I am certain my horse will win. Surely my certainty is in me, not in the horse. Suppose I doubt my lottery number will come up. Surely my doubt is in me, not in the number. Certainty about X and doubt about Y are not *features of* X and Y. Likewise, my certainty about my mind's existence is not a feature of my mind's existence, and my doubt about my body is not a feature of my body.

Many strange results could be produced if Descartes' argument about mind and body were valid. A child could prove, for example, that 2 + 2 does not equal 4. All the child needs to do is doubt that 2 + 2 does equal 4, while not doubting that 4 equals 4. Then the child could say, following Descartes:

1. I cannot be certain 2 + 2 = 4; and

2. I can be certain that 4 = 4; so,

3. 4 has a feature (being certainly equal to 4) that 2 + 2 lacks; but,

4. If X has a feature Y lacks, X ≠ Y; so,

5. 2 + 2 ≠ 4.

Since this argument has true premises and a false conclusion, it must be logically unsound; and if this argument is unsound, Descartes' argument must also be unsound. The mistake in both cases lies in step 3.

Third Argument Against Materialism: Each of Us Is an Authority on Our Own Mental States

The materialist believes each person's mind is identical with his or her brain. It follows that whoever knows best what is happening in my brain also knows best what is happening in my mind. This seems to go against common sense. A brain scientist may know better than I do what is happening in my brain, but I know better than any brain scientist what is happening in my own mind. For example, if I feel a pain, I know better than anyone in the world that I am in pain. I seem to have the ability, which no one else in the world has, to look into my own mind and see or feel what is going on there. I have "privileged access" to my own mental states. Materialism seems simply wrong when it claims a brain specialist could know about my pain better than I do, because he or she knows about my brain better than I do.

The Materialist Replies: We Know Our Minds No Better Than Our Brains

Philosophers have criticized the privileged access argument against materialism from two different directions. The first direction was suggested by the British philosopher Bertrand Russell, the second by his Austrian student Ludwig Wittgenstein.[3]

Objection 1. Is it really true we do not know what is happening in our own brains? I am not a brain specialist, but this does not show I know very little about *my own brain.* For materialists, mental states are brain states; and so, if I know my mental states, I automatically know my brain states. If I feel a pain, something must be happening in my brain; and if my pain changes, something in my brain must have changed. I know this as well as any brain specialist, because I am *hooked up* to my own brain in a way that nobody else is. My instruments for detecting what is happening in my brain—*my own nerves*—are better than any microscope. What the brain specialist knows about is *brains in general,* but it does not follow from this that the specialist knows about *my* brain events better than I do.

Objection 2. Are we really "authorities" on our mental states? When we are in pain, do we really *know* we are in pain? How do we know this? What did we do to find out? What justification can we give to support the claim that we are in pain? If I moan and groan, I could be faking. If I reply, "I just *feel* it," my "proof" that I feel a pain is that I feel a pain. This is like arguing that God exists because He exists. Certainly such arguments do not qualify as rational knowledge, still

---

[3] Neither Russell nor Wittgenstein believed in souls. But neither was a materialist. Philosophy is a complicated business.

less as perfect "authoritative" knowledge. Our alleged privileged access to our own minds is both a blessing and a curse. If we can't ever be wrong about our own mental states, then we can't be right either. Every claim to knowledge depends on a criterion that *distinguishes* being right from being wrong. Privileged access wipes out the criterion and destroys the possibility of the knowledge it was supposed to provide.

Fourth Argument Against Materialism: Mental States Have Intentionality

In 1874, the Austrian philosopher Franz Brentano (1838–1917) suggested that what makes mental states different from brain states is that mental events possess a property called *intentionality;* that is, mental states are all *about* something different from themselves. If I think about the Vietnam War, my thought is *about* the Vietnam War, which is the *object* of my thought. Brentano argued that the relation between thoughts and their objects is different from any physical relationship. Physical relationships can only exist between real physical things, but thoughts can have relations to objects that do not exist. When I think about Santa Claus, my thought is related to Santa Claus, who is the object of my thought. But none of my brain states is related to Santa Claus, because Santa Claus does not exist. Thoughts, then, must be different from brain states.

Another way of putting this is to say that thoughts, like words, have *meanings* that are different from themselves. No physical entity, however, has a meaning; no physical object is *about* anything. A table, by itself, simply is what it is. It has no meaning; it is "about" nothing. This suffices to show that tables—and brain states—are fundamentally different from thoughts.

The Materialist Replies: Intentionality Is an Ordinary Relation

Brentano believed *all* mental events have intentionality and *only* mental events have intentionality. Materialists argue that he was wrong on both counts.

Consider a feeling of pain, which is something almost all philosophers classify as a mental event. It is obviously a state of consciousness. Yet a feeling of pain has no object: it is not *about* anything. It simply is what it is, like a chair or a table. If pains are mental events, then not all mental events possess intentionality.

Now consider what happens when I see a table. Light bounces off the table and falls on my retina, which causes a chain of events in my optic nerve and eventually in my brain, which is my awareness of the table. What connects *my perception of the table* (in my brain) with *the table* (outside my brain) is the relation of cause and effect: the light bouncing off the table *caused* the event in my brain. What Brentano called the relation of intentionality is really the old-fashioned physical relationship of causation, and this relationship is not confined to the mental realm. When lightning causes thunder, we can, using Brentano's language, say that thunder is "about" lightning, or that thunder *means* lightning.

Brentano rejected the idea that intentionality was reducible to cause and effect. Cause and effect relations, however, can be very complicated, and they can do all the things Brentano thought intentionality could do. Consider Brentano's prime case: thinking about something that doesn't exist, like Santa Claus. Recall (from Part I) Russell's argument that so-called nonexistent things were simply sets of properties—that Santa Claus is just the combination of the properties *living at the North Pole, driving reindeer, wearing a red suit,* and so forth. My brain has already entered into cause and effect relationships with reindeer, redness, and the other properties that make up Santa Claus, because I have *seen* reindeer, red things, and so forth. When I think about Santa Claus, all I am doing is imagining all these properties are realized in one person living at the North Pole. Though Santa Claus is unreal, the properties that make up Santa Claus are physical and real. My thought about Santa Claus is a complicated thought about existing physical things.

Fifth Argument Against Materialism: Matter Is an Unwarranted Hypothesis

The four preceding arguments against materialism have assumed, without argument, that each human being has a physical body and that the nature of physical bodies is well understood. The fifth argument against materialism challenges these assumptions.

George Berkeley (1685–1753) issued the challenge in the eighteenth century. Berkeley, an Anglican bishop, fearing the bad effects of materialism on religion, set out to refute materialism by attacking its central concept: the concept of "material" or "physical" objects. According to materialism, a material object is supposed to be something that can exist even when no one is perceiving it. We all believe, for example, that the planets of the solar system would continue to exist even if there were a nuclear war that destroyed all life on Earth, leaving no one to observe the planets. By what right, asked Berkeley, do we assume the existence of such physical objects? By definition, matter is supposed to exist even if no one perceives it. But if no one perceives it, we have no way of verifying it is really there.

In science, we often make postulations about what we do not presently perceive, but afterward we expect to verify these postulations in the laboratory. The postulate of unperceived matter, however, is an assumption that can never be verified afterward. Berkeley concluded we have no right to postulate the existence of matter. In his view, the material world—the world of bodies, buildings, planets, stars, and galaxies that we suppose subsist outside of our minds—does not exist.

It would be a mistake to think that, in denying the existence of planets, stars, and galaxies *outside the mind,* Berkeley denied the existence of planets, stars, and galaxies *altogether.* On the contrary. Berkeley believed planets, stars, and galaxies *do* exist. But since they do not exist outside the mind, Berkeley reasoned they existed *inside* the mind. A star, according to Berkeley, is not an object that exists at a great distance from the mind; on the contrary, a star is a certain bundle of perceptions inside the mind: a little white dot against a black background in one's visual field. *To be,* said Berkeley, *is to be perceived.* This theory is called *idealism,* since it holds that the basic stuff from which reality is constructed is *ideas* in peoples' minds.

Many people since the eighteenth century have tried to refute Berkeley's philosophy, but it is not as easy to refute as one might think. The English author Samuel Johnson tried to refute Berkeley's theory by kicking a stone, reasoning that if stones were just bundles of perceptions, they could not collide with toes and cause pain.[4] But when Johnson kicked the stone and felt pain in his toe, all he succeeded in showing was that there is a connection between perceptions of stones and perceptions of pain. Consequently, he did not succeed in showing the stone existed outside of his mind.

Some have charged that if only perceptions exist, there will be no difference between dreams and reality. But Berkeley felt there were methods for distinguishing dreams from reality, even though dreams and reality are both made entirely of perceptions. The mind has in it many perceptions, but sometimes these perceptions are organized into groups and sometimes they are not. We call the perceptions that are organized into repeating groups or patterns "reality"; the perceptions that are not organized into repeating groups or patterns we call "dreams." After all, how *do* we tell the difference between dreams and reality? How do we know we are not dreaming right now? We tell dreams from reality by noticing that the events in dreams do not form any organized story that continues from day to day. If we ever had a dream with a continuous story, in which all events formed regular patterns, we would never know that it is a dream. In Berkeley's theory, such a dream, made of "bundles of ideas," would not be a dream. It would be reality itself.

The Materialist Replies: Matter Is a Reasonable Hypothesis

For Berkeley, to be is to be perceived, so we should spend some time thinking about perception. Suppose I see a table. There are two factors here: (1) my perceiving, which is an active process in my mind, and (2) the table as I perceive it, which Berkeley calls the "perception" or "idea." Now, which is it I perceive?

---

[4] Jonathan Swift gave Berkeley's theory even shorter shrift. When Berkeley called on Swift, Swift told the maid, "Don't open the door! Let him come through it."

For Berkeley, what I perceive is (2), the idea. It follows that I do *not* perceive (1), and, according to the rule that "to be is to be perceived," it follows that (1) does not exist. Berkeley's theory leads to the paradoxical result that everything is a perception, but the activity of perceiving does not exist.

According to Berkeley, objects are bundles of perceptions. Each person is a separate mind, and each bundle of perceptions can exist only in one mind. All persons, then, carry in their mind their own separate set of objects, their own universe. This leads to a problem. Why is my universe so much like other people's universes? Suppose 80,000 people attend a football game; the game is won on a field goal in the final seconds and 80,000 people shout at once. According to Berkeley's theory, there are 80,000 footballs going over 80,000 different goalposts. How is it that all the footballs happen to do the same thing at the same time? Berkeley's answer—that God arranges things so that the perceptions of different people are coordinated with each other—has satisfied few readers. Isn't it simpler and more reasonable to say 80,000 people shout at once because they all see *one* football, a physical object, going over a physical goalpost?

Sixth Argument Against Materialism: Robots Cannot Have Minds

For materialists, a human being is a physical object and human consciousness is a physical process. It follows from materialism that persons and their consciousness could be *constructed* from physical materials by mechanical means. Such mechanical people—for example, the robots R2-D2 and C3-PO in *Star Wars*—frequently appear in works of science fiction. The anti-materialist, however, claims that science fiction is science *fiction* and that the idea of a mechanical person is absurd. If I construct a toaster, the toaster has no consciousness. If I construct an automobile, the automobile is more complicated than the toaster, but it has no more consciousness than the toaster. I can go on building more and more complicated machines, but none of these machines will have any more consciousness than a toaster or an automobile. A metal and wire construction, however sophisticated, cannot perceive, feel, and think the way human beings do. Any doctrine like materialism that leads to the absurd claim that robots can be people or that computers can have consciousness must itself be absurd.

The Materialist Replies: Advanced Robots Will Have Minds

The sixth argument against materialism appeals to the idea that if simple things do not have consciousness, more complicated things of the same type cannot have consciousness. But if this argument is sound, *human beings* could not have consciousness. A human being starts from a fertilized egg, or *conceptus*. This conceptus then develops into an embryo, then a fetus, then a baby, by the biological processes of nutrition (absorption of chemicals from the surrounding fluid) and reproduction by fission. Now, a conceptus has no consciousness, and it does not seem possible for consciousness to develop from chemical absorption or fission reproduction. Yet it is a fact that babies can be conscious. Sometime during pregnancy consciousness must begin. The moral is that simple biological objects, like fertilized eggs, cannot have consciousness, but complicated biological objects, like babies, can. By parallel reasoning, we should think that though simple mechanical objects, like toasters, cannot have consciousness, complicated mechanical objects, like advanced computers, can.

At first, it is difficult to believe a computer, made of silicon chips and housed in a metal box, could have consciousness and be a person. But if the computer could hold a conversation with a human being, which is indistinguishable from the conversation of other human beings, then it would be reasonable to attribute consciousness to the computer. After all, we cannot experience any human being's consciousness except out own. We judge that other human beings have consciousness only because they speak and behave *as if they were* conscious. So if a robot, hidden behind a curtain, speaks and behaves as if it were conscious, it would be human "protein prejudice" to deny that the robot is conscious just because its brain is made of silicon chips. It follows that computers can have minds and robots could be people.

Seventh Argument Against Materialism: The Mental Emerges from the Physical

The materialist maintains that everything is made of matter. But, as Berkeley asked, "What is matter?" For centuries materialists have answered this question by appealing to the science of physics. In the late twentieth century, the answer provided by physics is that matter consists of *elementary particles* like quarks, electrons, and photons. The activities of these particles are governed by three *elementary forces:* (1) the strong force, which controls events in the atomic nucleus; (2) the electroweak force, which governs radioactive decay and the interactions of charged particles; and (3) the force of gravity. *Physical phenomena,* then, are all the things implied by the existence of elementary particles and the three forces that control them. Now, if we look around the universe, we discover there are many phenomena that cannot be explained simply by referring to elementary particles and the three forces that control them. Therefore, we should conclude that *some phenomena are not physical phenomena.*

These nonphysical phenomena are not strange, mystical events. They are as familiar as the properties of chemical compounds. Consider hydrogen and oxygen. If we knew everything about hydrogen and everything about oxygen, we still would not be able to know or predict that when hydrogen joins with oxygen it makes something wet. The properties of water are remarkably different from the properties of hydrogen and oxygen. Since we cannot deduce them from the properties of atoms, they are not physical phenomena. What are they? They are chemical phenomena.

What we should say is that the properties of water "emerge" from the properties of hydrogen and oxygen. And chemistry is not the only example of emergence. If we knew everything that could be known about chemical compounds, we would not be able to predict that some chemical compounds could get together to form a living thing. *Biological* properties emerge from chemical properties. Similarly, if we knew everything that could be known about the cells that form a human brain, we would not be able to predict that those cells working together could produce thoughts, learn a language, develop theories, or create works of art. *Psychological* properties emerge from biological properties: mind emerges from brain. When the first chemical compounds came into existence, some thousands of years after the Big Bang, something entirely new came into the universe. Likewise, when life began three and a half billion years ago, or when symbol-using creatures evolved several hundred thousand years ago, something entirely new came into the universe.

Hence, to say "human beings are nothing but matter" is misleading. Human beings *contain* matter, but the properties human beings possess, especially the property of having a mind, are distinct from any properties that matter alone has. The psychological is *not reducible* to the physical; the mind is not reducible to the brain.

One way to understand this lack of "reducibility" is to consider a prosaic example: The game of baseball. The rules of baseball define its key concepts: a *home run* is roughly defined as a baseball being hit over the outfield fence within the foul lines and so forth. This definition makes it sound as if a home run is a simple physical event: a physical object making an arc through space. But a home run is *not* just an object making an arc through space: it is an object making an arc through space *while a game of baseball is being played.* Home runs can only happen when there are people playing according to rules, knowing the rules, and intending to play by them. No motion of a ball in the seventeenth century could be a home run: the game had not been invented yet. So we should say that a home run is "not reducible to" the physical motion of a ball. In much the same way, the psychological is not reducible to the physical: thoughts are to brain events as home runs are to balls hit over the fence during baseball games.

The Materialist Replies: Emergence Is an Illusion Created by Theories

Let us take a careful look at the example of the home run. What makes a home run different from the simple physical motion of a ball going over a fence? Obviously, it is that home runs happen when baseball games are being played. And what does it take to play a baseball game? It takes people, people who know the rules and who play according to the rules. Thus, a home run will "emerge" from a moving baseball only if human minds exist to interpret the motion of the ball according to the rules of the game. There are not two things—the ball's motion *and* the home run—but only one thing—the motion of the ball, which is sometimes *interpreted* as being a home run. Emergence is an illusion created by interpretation.

Just as home runs are the results of interpretation, the physical, the chemical, the biological, and the psychological are the results of interpretation. What we call the physical realm is simply the world interpreted according to the theories of physics. Similarly, the chemical realm is the world interpreted according to the theories of chemistry. Physical theories and chemical theories may be different, but they are both about the same material world. Likewise, theories of human biology and theories of human psychology may be different, but they are both about the same thing: the living human body, including the brain.

A Final Plea for Reincarnation

In the preceding sections, we have reviewed many criticisms of materialism. Suppose the criticisms fail and materialism is true. That is sufficient to refute the pure soul theory: the idea that a person could have consciousness without having any body or brain. But the success of materialism does not refute the basic idea of reincarnation, because reincarnation does not assert that persons can exist without bodies. In fact, most advocates of reincarnation say, just as materialists do, that every person has a body at every moment of his or her life. According to reincarnation teaching, though you may not have the *same* body, you always have *a* body.

Even the requirement that persons must *remember* something of their former lives provides no unsolvable problem for reincarnation theory. Suppose we assume, like good materialists, that a *memory* is a certain kind of state in a person's brain: a pattern in the brain neurons. When a person dies, those neurons die, but it is possible the same *pattern* of neurons could exist in a new brain, in which case that new brain would have the same memories as the brain of the person who died. By the criteria of personal identity, then, the new brain would be the brain of the same person as the person who died. He or she would be the same person *reincarnated*.

Last Words Against Reincarnation

There are arguments against reincarnation that do not depend on materialism. Here are two.

1. The basic idea of reincarnation is that the same person can have different

bodies at different times. But if it is possible for the same person to have two different bodies at two different times, it must be possible for the same person to have two bodies *at the same time*. If a memory is a pattern of neurons, then it is possible for two bodies at the same time to have the same pattern of neurons and the same memories. In such a case, there would be *one* person at *one* time with *two* bodies. That person could meet himself or herself walking down the street! But this is an absurd result, and the theory that produced it must be equally absurd.

2. Reincarnation theory assumes that the same person can live, century after century, in body after body. But consider the relationship that will exist between my present incarnation in the twentieth century and my future incarnation in the thirtieth century. That incarnation, 1,000 years hence, will have only the vaguest memories of my life;[5] his personality will be different; his body will be different; and there is no reason to believe he will have any relationships with the future incarnations of my present friends and relatives. By what stretch of the imagination is that future incarnation *me*? Is that incarnation what people hope for when they hope for a life after death? Do we really care whether we have an incarnation in the thirtieth century? Our concept of human life is geared in myriad ways to the idea that we live for less than 100 years. The concept of a life that lasts for 1,000 years is not the concept of a *human* life at all. Perhaps there are immortal beings, but these immortal beings cannot be human beings.

Would Eternal Life Be a Good Thing?

Most people in Western countries assume that eternal life would be a good thing. They are surprised to discover that eternal life is viewed as an evil in many cultures. Hindus, for example, feel that to be reborn over and over again is a great evil, even if in most reincarnations one experiences a comfortable life. The supreme good in Hinduism is not the preservation of the self but its complete annihilation in the selfless awareness called "Nirvana." This attitude of the Hindus applies to the pure soul theory as well. If our souls survive death and go on perceiving for eternity, if we cannot ever escape from personal consciousness, then eternal life might be a burden even if we perceive pleasant things.

If we live forever, we must be able to remember our past experiences. If we could not, then we would lose our personal identity across time and not have eternal life. But if we live for eternity and remember our past experiences, our minds will be burdened with millions of memories. Nothing we perceive will ever be new and fresh.

If we do *not* live forever, then every moment is precious because it is one of the few we have. Every experience can be fresh because it can be different

---

[5] He will remember some previous incarnation, who in turn remembers an incarnation . . . who remembers an incarnation who remembers my present life.

from what we have had before. True, our sequence of experiences will come to an end with death, but the fact that our experiences will come to an end cannot deprive them of the value they have for us when we are alive. Perhaps what matters most is not how *long* we live, but how *well* we live. Living well is the subject of Part III.

SUGGESTIONS FOR FURTHER READING

The Concept of Life After Death

For problems in the definition of death, see Tom Beauchamp and Seymour Perlin, eds., *Ethical Issues in Death and Dying* (Englewood Cliffs, N.J.: Prentice-Hall, 1978), and James Bernat, Charles Culver, and Bernard Gert, "Defining Death in Theory and Practice," *Hastings Center Report* (March 1982).

For analyses of personal identity, see the articles in John Perry, ed., *Personal Identity** (Berkeley: University of California Press, 1975), and Amelie Oksenberg Rorty, ed., *The Identities of Persons** (Berkeley: University of California Press, 1976); see also, Kathleen V. Wilkes, *Real People: Personal Identity Without Thought Experiments* (New York: Oxford University Press, 1988).

For analyses of the logical problems involved in the pure soul theory, see Terence Penelhum, *Survival and Disembodied Existence* (New York: Humanities Press, 1970), and Anthony Flew, *The Logic of Mortality* (Oxford: Basil Blackwell, 1987). For the logical problems involved in reincarnation, see C. J. Ducasse, *The Belief in Life After Death* (Springfield, Ill.: Thomas, 1961, Chs. 20 and 21), and Derek Parfit, *Reasons and Persons** (New York: Oxford University Press, 1984, Part III).

For special problems involved in the Christian doctrine of resurrection, see George Mavrodes, "The Life Everlasting and the Bodily Criterion of Identity," *Nous* (1977), and Peter Van Inwagen, "The Possibility of Resurrection," *International Journal for the Philosophy of Religion* (1978).

Must We Die Before We Know?

Post-death or far-future verifications are sometimes called "eschatological verifications." See Robert Audi, "Eschatological Verification and Personal Identity," *International Journal for the Philosophy of Religion* (1976).

First Argument for Life After Death: Near-Death Experiences

For near-death experiences, see Raymond Moody, *Life After Life* (Atlanta, Ga.: Mockingbird Press, 1975), and I. Osis and E. Haraldsson, *At the Hour of Death* (New York: Avon, 1977). A similar near-death experience recently unsettled A. J. Ayer, one of the century's most tough-minded philosophers; see John Ezard, "Ayer's Thoughts from the Other Side," *Manchester Guardian* (September 11, 1988).

---

* Asterisk denotes an advanced technical discussion.

Criticism of Reports of Near-Death Experiences

See James E. Adcock, "Psychology and Near Death Experiences," *The Sceptical Inquirer* (Spring 1979).

Second Argument for Life After Death: Memories of Former Lives

For reports of memories of former lives, see C. J. Ducasse, *The Belief in Life After Death*, Ch. 23; Ian Stevenson, *Twenty Cases Suggestive of Reincarnation* (Charlottesville: University of Virginia Press, 1974); Ian Stevenson, *Unlearned Language: New Studies in Xenoglossy* (Charlottesville: University of Virginia Press, 1984); Jeffrey Iverson, *More Lives Than One?* (London: Pan Books, 1977); and Helen Wambach, *Reliving Past Lives: The Evidence Under Hypnosis* (New York: Harper and Row, 1978).

For the Bridey Murphy case, see Morey Bernstein, *The Search for Bridey Murphy* (Garden City, N.Y.: Doubleday, 1956), and C. J. Ducasse, *The Belief in Life After Death*, Ch. 25.

Criticism of Alleged Memories of Former Lives

For analysis of the Bridey Murphy case, see M. V. Kline, ed., *A Scientific Report on the Search for Bridey Murphy* (New York: Julian Press, 1956), and Marvin Harris, "Are Past Life Regressions Evidence for Reincarnation?" *Free Inquiry* 6.4 (1986).

Third Argument for Life After Death: Communication with the Dead

For reports of spirit communications, see C. D. Broad, *Lectures on Psychical Research* (London: Routledge and Kegan Paul, 1962, Section C); Colin Wilson, *Afterlife* (Garden City, N.Y.: Doubleday, 1985); and Robert Almeder, *Beyond Death* (Springfield, Ill.: Thomas, 1987).

Criticism of Reports of Communication with the Dead

See C. J. Ducasse, *The Belief in Life After Death*, Part IV: Ronald Pearsall, *The Table Rappers* (New York: St. Martin's Press, 1973); and C. E. M. Hansel, *ESP and Parapsychology: A Critical Evaluation* (Buffalo, N.Y.: Prometheus Press, 1984, Part I).

For the question of "unlearned languages," see Sarah Thomason, "Past Tongues," *The Sceptical Inquirer* (Summer 1987).

Some Further Problems in Proofs of Immortality

These points are made by C. D. Broad, *The Mind and Its Place in Nature* (London: Routledge and Kegan Paul, 1925, Chs. 11 and 12).

Fourth Argument for Life After Death: God Will Provide

A similar argument is developed in Hindu theology for the existence of reincarnation. The universe has a moral order, and a moral order demands that the wicked be made to suffer. But many wicked people die happily in their beds. It must be, then, that these wicked people are punished in their future lives. For texts, see R. C. Zaehner, *Hinduism* (Oxford: Oxford University Press, 1962).

Criticism: Even the Good Do Not Deserve Salvation

The theme that nobody deserves to be saved is prominent in Augustinian theology. See Martin Luther, *Free Will and Salvation,* E. Gordon Rupp, trans. (Philadelphia: Westminster, 1969).

First Argument Against Life After Death: Evolution Implies Mortality

The argument that it is absurd to deny immortality to lower animals while admitting it for humans was developed without help from the theory of evolution by Hume, "On the Immortality of the Soul," in *Essays: Moral, Political, Literary* (Indianapolis, Ind.: Liberty Fund, 1985, pp. 590–98). For a more modern presentation, see Bertrand Russell, "What I Believe," in Paul Edwards, ed., *Why I am Not a Christian* (New York: Simon and Schuster, 1957).

For an optimistic account of life elsewhere in the universe, see I. S. Shklovskii and Carl Sagan, *Intelligent Life in the Universe* (New York: Dell, 1966). For relatively more somber reflections, see Robert Schapiro and Gerald Feinberg, *Life Beyond Earth* (New York: Morrow, 1980).

Criticism: Thought Is More Fundamental Than Any Physical Process

The argument that only humans have language is affirmed by several essays in Thomas Sebeok and Jean Umiker-Sebok, eds., *Speaking of Apes* (New York: Continuum, 1980).

The argument concerning the primacy of thought is made famous in Descartes' *Discourse on Method* [1637]:

This mind, which makes me what I am, is totally distinct from my body, is more easily known than my body, and . . . would continue to be all that it is, even if my body did not exist.

Second Argument Against Life After Death: Consciousness Depends on Brain Processes

For arguments that even if thoughts are not physical they depend on the physical, see Thomas Huxley, "On the Physical Basis of Life: Method and Results," in *Collected Essays* (London: Macmillan, 1898), and Broad, *Mind and Its Place in Nature.*

Criticism: A Report of Deep Sleep May Be Mistaken

The idea that one's body could be dormant while one's mind is active is supported by reports of "out of the body experiences"; see Robert Monroe, *Journey Out of the Body* (New York: Doubleday, 1971).

Third Argument Against Life After Death: Thoughts Are Themselves Physical (The Thesis of Materialism)

Classic presentations of materialism include Lucretius, *De Rerum Natura* [ca. 60 B.C.]; Thomas Hobbes, *De Corpore* [1640]; Julien Offray La Mettrie, *L'Homme Machine* [1738]; and Paul Heinrich Dietrich d'Holbach, *System de la Nature* [1770]. Modern presentations include Paul Feyerabend, "Materialism and the Mind-Body Problem,"* *Review of Metaphysics* (1963), and D. H. Armstrong, *A Materialist Theory of the Mind** (London: Routledge and Kegan Paul, 1968).

First Argument for Materialism: Mind-Brain Correlations

For a review of current information about mind-brain correlations (or the lack of them), see Howard Gardiner, *The Mind's New Science* (New York: Basic Books, 1985, Ch. 9); Patricia S. Churchland, *Neurophilosophy** (Cambridge, Mass.: MIT Press, 1986); Neil Stillings, et al., *Cognitive Science: An Introduction* (Cambridge, Mass: MIT Press, 1987); and Patricia S. Churchland and T. J. Sejnowski, "Perspectives on Cognitive Neuroscience,"* *Science* (November 4, 1988): 741–45.

Criticism: Correlations Do Not Prove Identity

For a very sophisticated version of this argument, which depends on the thesis that if mind states were brain states it must be *impossible* to have one without the other, see Saul Kripke, *Naming and Necessity** (Cambridge, Mass.: Harvard University Press, 1982, 144–55).

Second Argument for Materialism: Interaction Between Mind and Body

The difficulties of explaining soul-body interaction are a principal theme of seventeenth-century philosophy. See, for example, Descartes, *Meditation* VI, and the correspondence between Hobbes (materialist) and Descartes (anti-materialist) in "Objections and Replies" to Descartes' *Meditations,* E. S. Haldane and G. T. R. Ross, trans., *Philosophical Works of Descartes* Vol. II (New York: Dover Publications, 1955).

Criticism: Causation Does Not Require Contact

The idea that causation does not require contact, that there can be "action at a distance," was introduced in 1686 by Isaac Newton as part of his theory of universal gravitation. See Florian Cajori, ed., *Isaac Newton's Mathematical Principles of Natural Philosophy and His System of the World** (Berkeley: University of California Press, 1966). David Hume's analysis of causation is most lucidly presented in his *Philosophical Essays Concerning Human Understanding* [1748], Ch. 7.

In addition to the arguments in the succeeding sections, the student would do well to consider the anti-materialistic threads in Donald Davidson, "Mental Events,"* and "The Material Mind,"* in *Essays on Action and Events* (New York: Oxford University Press, 1980), and Thomas Nagel, *The View from Nowhere* (New York: Oxford University Press, 1986).

First Argument Against Materialism: Thoughts Lack Physical Properties

For a comprehensive review of these issues, see Herbert Feigl, *The "Mental" and the "Physical"* (Minneapolis: University of Minnesota Press, 1967).

The Materialist Replies: Thoughts Are Events, Not Objects

For thoughts as events, see J. J. C. Smart, *Philosophy and Scientific Realism* (London: Routledge and Kegan Paul, 1963). For a different materialist account of why the agony of a pain is not a property of the pain, see James Cornman, *Materialism and Sensations** (New Haven, Conn.: Yale University Press, 1970).

Second Argument Against Materialism: Descartes and Doubt

Descartes develops this argument in his *Discourse on Method* [1637] and *Meditations* I and II [1641]. W. D. Hart, *The Engines of the Soul* (Cambridge: Cambridge University Press, 1988), gives the argument a modern defense.

The Materialist Replies: Certainty About X Is Not a Feature of X

The error of Descartes' argument is that it relies on the principle that equals can always be substituted for equals; for example, 4 can always be substituted for 2 + 2. For discussion of failures of the principle of substitution, see Leonard Linsky, *Referring** (London: Routledge and Kegan Paul, 1967).

Third Argument Against Materialism: Each of Us Is an Authority on Our Own Mental States

For elaboration, see Richard Rorty, "Incorrigibility as the Mark of the Mental," *Journal of Philosophy* (1970), and Raziel Abelson, *Persons: A Study in Philosophical Psychology* (New York: St. Martin's Press, 1977).

The Materialist Replies: We Know Our Minds No Better Than Our Brains

The argument in Objection 1 is made by Michael Levin, *Materialism and the Mind-Body Problem** (Oxford: Oxford University Press, 1979). The argument in Objection 2 is a version of a famous argument from Ludwig Wittgenstein called "the private language argument." Despite its name, this is an argument that there can be *no such thing* as a private language and therefore no such thing as "private knowledge," expressed in a private language, of one's own mental states. See Wittgenstein, *Philosophical Investigations** (New York: Macmillan, 1953, Sections 258–74). For exegesis, see Norman Malcom, *Knowledge and Certainty* (Englewood Cliffs, N.J.: Prentice-Hall, 1963, pp. 96–129).

Fourth Argument Against Materialism: Mental States Have Intentionality

For Brentano, see, Linda McAlister et al., trans., *Psychology from an Empirical Standpoint** [1874] (New York: Humanities Press, 1973).

For a modern discussion of intentionality, see the correspondence between Roderick Chisholm and Wilfrid Sellars, reprinted in *Minnesota Studies in the Philosophy of Science,* Vol. II (Minneapolis: University of Minnesota Press, 1958): Daniel Dennett, *Content and Consciousness** (London: Routledge and Kegan Paul, 1969, Ch. 2); Hubert Dreyfus, *What Computers Can't Do* (New York: Harper and Row, 1979); and Daniel Dennett, *The Intentional Stance** (Cambridge, Mass.: MIT Press, 1987).

The Materialist Replies: Intentionality Is an Ordinary Relation

For an analysis of "intentionality" that asserts that intentionality can be a physical relation, see John Searle, *Intentionality* New York: Cambridge University Press, 1983).

Fifth Argument Against Materialism: Matter Is an Unwarranted Hypothesis

Berkeley's system is presented in two delightful books: *A Treatise Concerning the Principles of Human Knowledge* [1710] and *Three Dialogues Between Hylas and Philonous* [1713]. Various paperback editions are available. For a modern argument that the concept of material object can be replaced by the concept of a bundle of perceptions, see Bertrand Russell, *Our Knowledge of the External World* (London: Allen and Unwin, 1914).

The Materialist Replies: Matter Is a Reasonable Hypothesis

Classic repudiations of Berkeley's theory include Thomas Reid, *An Inquiry into the Human Mind and the Principles of Common Sense* [1764]; Immanuel Kant, "Refutation of Idealism,"* *Critique of Pure Reason,* 275–279 [1787]; and G. E. Moore, "A Refutation of Idealism" [1903], *Philosophical Studies* (London: Routledge and Kegan Paul, 1922).

The argument that material objects provide the best hypotheses for explaining the conformity of perception among different people is given by Bertrand Russell, *The Analysis of Matter** (New York: Harcourt Brace and World, 1927, Ch. 20).

Sixth Argument Against Materialism: Robots Cannot Have Minds

Arguments that computers cannot possess consciousness or knowledge are given in John Searle, "Minds, Brains, and Programs," *Behavioral and Brain Sciences* (1980), and *Minds, Brains, and Science* (Cambridge, Mass.: Harvard University Press, 1984). See also, J. Weizbaum, *Computer Power and Human Reason* (San Francisco: W. H. Freeman, 1976).

The Materialist Replies: Advanced Robots Will Have Minds

The argument that advanced robots could be people is cleverly laid out in Justin Leiber, *Can Animals and Machines Be Persons?* (Indianapolis, Ind.: Hackett, 1985). See also, John Pollack, "My Brother, the Machine,"* *Nous* (1988).

The argument that any entity that could respond to questions in a manner indistinguishable from a human being must be said to have a mind is set out in Alan Turing, "Computing Machinery and Intelligence," *Mind* (1950). For a related argument, see Michael Scriven, "The Compleat Robot," in Sidney Hook, ed., *Dimensions of Mind* (New York: New York University Press, 1960).

The view that the computer (or a set of computer programs) provides the best model of the human mind is called *functionalism*. For presentations of functionalism, see the papers by Hilary Putnam reprinted as Chapters 14, 18, 19, 20, and 21 in Putnam, *Philosophical Papers, Vol. II.: Mind, Language, and Reality** (New York: Cambridge University Press, 1975). For criticisms of functionalism, see Ned Block, "Troubles with Functionalism,"* *Minnesota Studies in the Philosophy of Science* (1978), and Putnam's retractions in *Representation and Reality** (Cambridge, Mass.: MIT Press, 1988, Chs. 5 and 6). Note that functionalism does not imply materialism: the "computers" discussed by functionalists could be made from spiritual stuff. Functionalism, however, *does* imply that thinking physical objects are possible.

Seventh Argument Against Materialism: The Mental Emerges from the Physical

For a general cosmology of emergence, see Samuel Alexander, *Space, Time, and Deity* (London: Macmillan, 1920). A more recent example is Karl Popper and John Eccles, *The Self and Its Brain* (New York: Springer-Verlag, 1977). For criticisms, see P. E. Meehl and Wilfrid Sellars, "The Concept of Emergence,"* *Minnesota Studies in the Philosophy of Science* Vol. I (1956).

For arguments that social entities like home runs cannot be reduced to physical entities and processes see G. E. M. Anscombe, *Intention** (Oxford: Basil Blackwell, 1957).

The Materialist Replies: Emergence Is an Illusion Created by Theories

For arguments that multiple interpretations of physical processes are compatible with the general program of materialism, see Edgar Wilson, *The Mental as Physical** (London: Routledge and Kegan Paul, 1979, Ch. 4).

A Final Plea for Reincarnation

The crucial question for this argument is whether the same pattern of neurons in the new brain is the same memory or a new memory that is very similar to the old one. For critical discussion of whether the same person could have a new body, see John Perry, *Dialogue on Personal Identity and Immortality* (Indianapolis, Ind.: Hackett, 1978); David Wiggins, *Sameness and Substance** (Oxford: Basil Blackwell, 1980); and Derek Parfit, *Reasons and Persons** (New York: Oxford University Press, 1984, Part III).

Last Words Against Reincarnation

Some of the problems in the idea of a 1,000-year human life are discussed in Bernard Williams, "The Makroupolous Case: Reflections on the Tedium of Immortality," in his *Problems of the Self* (New York: Cambridge University Press, 1973).

Would Eternal Life Be a Good Thing?

The dreary side of eternal life is articulated by C. D. Broad, *Lectures on Psychical Research,* Epilogue, and Bernard Williams, "The Makroupolous Case." The problem of maintaining zest in the face of endlessly repeated experiences is a main theme of Friedrich Nietzsche, *Thus Spake Zarathustra,* in Walter Kaufman, trans., *The Portable Nietzsche* (New York: Viking, 1969, pp. 330–31).

Freedom and Morality

Scepticism About Ethics

From the earliest times people have been interested in questions of ethics. What makes life worth living? What are my moral obligations? What is the relationship between a rational life and a moral life? These are serious questions, Plato said, because they concern how to live.

Over the centuries philosophers, religious teachers, and political leaders have developed and presented solutions to ethical problems. They have assumed that ethical questions *do* have answers and that these answers can be justified.

Some philosophers, however, have denied this assumption. These *ethical sceptics* believe there are no rationally justifiable ethical opinions. But is such scepticism *itself* rationally justifiable? We will begin with three arguments that support scepticism about ethics.

First Challenge to Ethics: Determinism

In his *Critique of Practical Reason* (1788), Kant articulated the famous claim that *"ought" implies "can."* What Kant meant was that every judgment that a person *ought* to do action A implies he *can* do action A. It follows from Kant's principle that a person cannot be morally responsible for an action if it was the only thing he or she could do at the time. By itself, Kant's principle presents no problems for ethics. But trouble arises when Kant's principle is combined with another philosophical doctrine: *determinism*.

Determinism is the claim that *every event has a cause*. These causes operate according to laws, and thus the conditions of the universe at each moment determine precisely what will happen at the next. According to determinism, whenever a person does something, there was a condition of the universe that made him or her do it.

Thus, while Kant says

1.   Jones is morally blameable for doing act A (at time *t*) only if there was an alternative act B that Jones could have done (at *t*),

determinism says

2.   Jones had no alternative to doing A (at *t*).

It follows from 1 and 2 that Jones is not morally blameable for A or for any other act. No person is ever to blame for anything. If so, moral criticism of human actions is pointless. Whenever a person's actions are criticized, he or she can always reply, "I couldn't help it."

Determinists feel that solid evidence for their doctrine is provided by physics. The human body is a piece of matter, and the motion of an object the size of a human body is governed by two physical forces: gravity and electromagnetism. Given the forces acting on the body, it cannot move any other way than the way it does move.

Just as the motions of the body are governed by physical laws, the mind's choices are governed by psychological laws. A person at every moment will have certain desires, and the sum of these desires will determine what a person chooses to do. Given these desires, he or she could not choose to do anything else.

Furthermore, the desires people have are a result of the kind of persons they are, and the kind of persons they are results from their heredity and their environment. Given their heredity and environment, they could not have different desires than the ones they have. People do not freely choose their desires, and therefore they do not freely choose their actions. What philosophers call "free will" does not exist.

For these reasons, then, all human actions are predetermined and none is blameable. Belief in free will and belief in ethics are superstitions, relics of an earlier unscientific age.

The Moralist's Reply to Determinism

Let us call people who believe ethics is *not* a superstition *moralists*. Moralists dispute every point in the determinist's challenge to ethics.

Is Kant's Principle True? Kant's principle says "ought" implies "can," but this principle can be questioned. Consider the following examples:

1.   Jones is in a room that has one door and one window. Jones believes the door is unlocked, but decides to exit through the window, deliberately smashing the glass in the process.

Surely Jones is morally responsible for breaking the glass, *even if,* unknown to Jones, the door and window are both actually locked; and, in fact, he has *no other way* of getting out of the room except by smashing the window. In this case, Jones is morally responsible for breaking the window, even though, unknown to him, he had no alternative but to break it.

2.   Jones has been thinking about killing his wife, Ethel, but hasn't yet decided whether he will do it. Unknown to him, Svengali, the world's greatest hypnotist, also wants Ethel dead. Should Jones choose not to kill Ethel, Svengali will hypnotize Jones and make him, while hypnotized, kill her anyway. Jones, on his own, chooses to kill Ethel, and Svengali does nothing.

Isn't Jones responsible for Ethel's death? Isn't he a full-fledged murderer, even though it was inevitable that he would kill her anyway?

These are strange examples, but they prove a point. If we agree that Jones is morally responsible for breaking the window, and for killing Ethel, then we must reject Kant's principle. For we are saying that Jones ought not to have broken the window, even though he could not avoid breaking it, and that he ought not to have killed his wife, even though he could not avoid killing her. It seems that having alternatives is not necessary for the existence of moral responsibility, and determinism and moral responsibility are *compatible.* Philosophers who hold this view are called "compatibilists."

When, according to compatibilism, are people morally responsible for their acts? Many compatibilists have suggested that we should presume people are responsible, *unless* they have a good excuse for doing what they did. The theory of moral responsibility, for compatibilists, is simply the theory of good excuses.

Different compatibilists, however, have proposed different lists of excuses. The list proposed by Aristotle, one of the first philosophers to study moral responsibility in depth, provides a good starting point for the understanding of compatibilism.

In Aristotle's account, persons have only two valid excuses by which they can avoid blame: *ignorance* and *compulsion.* A person is not morally responsible for doing A if he did not know he was doing A: for example, he is not responsible for poisoning a man if he had good reason to believe he was giving him medicine. That is the excuse of ignorance. Likewise, a person is not morally responsible for doing A if he was forced to do A: for example, a sea captain is not responsible for falling behind schedule if a hurricane blows his boat off course. That is the excuse of compulsion. Notice that it is specific ignorance of facts that excuses: for Aristotle, ignorance of the moral law provides no excuse. And notice that the compulsion that excuses is entirely external: there is no condoning in Aristotle of what today we call "compulsive behavior."

Some familiar excuses are specifically *rejected* by Aristotle; in fact, to offer them is a sign of bad character. For example, Aristotle in general did not accept *coercion* as an excuse: if a tyrant demands a shameful act, in most cases a person is morally responsible if he does not resist the tyrant. But Aristotle adds, quite reasonably:

On some actions, praise indeed is not bestowed, but pardon is, as when one does a wrongful act under pressure which overstrains human nature and which no one could withstand.

Aristotle also rejects *passion* as an excuse: if a person acts from great anger, he is responsible, because an adult should have the ability to control his emotions. Likewise, Aristotle would reject *heredity and environment* as excuses, since he views personal character as a set of habits developed over many years through the performance of acts that are themselves voluntary. Finally, Aristotle rejects *addiction* as an excuse: if a person breaks a law because he is too drunk to help himself, his drunkenness does not constitute an excuse, even if it is chronic, since chronic drunkenness is itself a sign of bad character. In cases of drunken lawbreaking, Aristotle said, the fine should be *double*.

Readers should review each of the excuses discussed here to see if they agree with Aristotle, or whether they are prepared to add coercion, passion, heredity, environment, addiction—or other things, like mental illness—to the list of good excuses that exonerate a person from moral responsibility. But according to compatibilism what makes an excuse valid has nothing to do with whether the action in question was caused or uncaused. It also has nothing to do with whether the person who performed the action could have done something else.

Is Determinism True? Determinists say that all events have causes and are produced according to strict physical laws. But quantum physics maintains that the laws of physics do not determine the events that occur within atoms; on the contrary, it holds that many events that occur within atoms occur spontaneously. Furthermore, if chemical and biological phenomena *emerge* from physical phenomena, chemical and biological events are not determined by the laws of physics. Thus it is not true, as determinism claims, that the conditions of the universe at one moment determine precisely what will happen at the next. Given conditions in the universe one month after the Big Bang, life did not exist, and it was not predetermined then that life would ever come to be.

Determinists say people will always choose to do what they most desire to do. But if determinism is scientific, we must evaluate this claim by scientific standards. Scientific standards require that every hypothesis be tested as to whether it can make successful predictions. If a hypothesis fails to make successful predictions, it is no part of science.

Can the claim that "everyone does what he most desires to do," be used to make successful predictions? Suppose Jane is told she must donate a kidney to her sister or else her sister will die from kidney disease. Jane feels she ought to help her sister. On the other hand, she finds the prospect of surgery disgusting and frightening. Will she have the surgery? Does the theory that "everyone does what he most desires to do" help us one bit in predicting what Jane will do? Not at all. Since it cannot help with predictions, the theory is not good science.

Determinists say a person's wishes and desires are the product of heredity and environment. No one could deny that heredity and environment have a great influence on personality and behavior, but there is a big difference between saying heredity and environment *influence* behavior and saying heredity and environment *determine* behavior. Given Jane's heredity and upbringing, it is perhaps 90 percent probable she will donate one kidney to her sister. But if heredity and environment determine behavior, then, whatever she does, it must have been 100 percent probable she would do it. Few people believe heredity and environment have *that* much influence. One can know everything about hydrogen and everything about oxygen and still not know that when hydrogen and oxygen get together, the two will produce something wet. Likewise, one can know everything about hereditary influences and everything about environmental influences and still not know that, when *this* heredity and *this* environment get together, the result will be someone like Jane.

Second Challenge to Ethics: Ethical Relativism

Everyone knows that different cultures have different moral codes. Hindus think it is morally permissible to eat pork but not permissible to eat beef; Moslems think it is permissible to eat beef but not permissible to eat pork. Hindus believe their code is true and the Moslem code is false; Moslems think exactly the reverse. *Ethical relativism* says that all cultural codes are equally valid. It follows that a claim like "it is immoral to eat beef" is neither true nor false. What we can say is that it is immoral *in the Hindu code,* but we cannot say that the Hindu code is true.

According to ethical relativism, when moralists claim a certain moral judgment is *true*—true for *everyone*—they forget that moral codes are simply cultural products, the results of history and custom. When people claim their own moral judgments are *true*, they are presuming that their own cultural code is superior—"closer to the truth"—than other cultural codes. This attitude was common in the nineteenth century, when European writers assumed that European morals were more civilized, more "true," than non-European morals. This prejudice in favor of European morals is the unsavory equivalent of imperialism in politics and racism in anthropology. The truth is not that one culture's morals are better than another's, but that all cultures are equally worthy of respect.

The Moralist's Reply to Ethical Relativism

Ethical relativists base their case on alleged deep differences between the codes of different cultures. But according to the moralist, the most important rules in the codes of different cultures are not that different. All cultures, for example, have some rules forbidding indiscriminate killing, stealing, and other such actions that, left unregulated, would tear the culture apart.

Furthermore, even if there are fundamental differences in moral codes among the world's cultures, this by itself cannot prove that all codes are equally valid. After all, different cultures have different *scientific* views, but we do not infer from these differences that all scientific views are equally valid. Some cultures hold that the earth is round; others hold that the earth is flat. We do not, however, conclude from this disagreement that the earth is round in one culture and flat in another. Thus, a *mere* difference of codes proves nothing about the validity of the codes.

When relativists argue that "all codes are equally worthy of respect," they refute their own position. Such a rule applies to *all* cultures, so this rule, at least, *cannot* be culturally relative. If relativists argue that all cultures deserve respect, then there is at least one objective truth of ethics: the truth that all cultures deserve respect.

Third Challenge to Ethics: Emotivism

In the preceding section, the moralist argued that cultural differences in ethics were similar to cultural differences in science. Philosophers called *emotivists* argue that this comparison is mistaken. According to emotivism, a scientific claim can be proven by experiments; a moral claim cannot be proven by experiments. A true scientific claim corresponds to an objective reality that exists outside of people's minds. A moral claim does not correspond to an objective reality outside of people's minds. Thus, scientific claims are *either* true or false; ethical claims are *neither* true nor false.

According to emotivists, the reason ethical claims cannot correspond to an objective reality is that ethical claims express feelings, rather than describing facts. When people say a killing was "bloody," they base their claim on sense perception, but when they say the same killing was "wicked" they are merely expressing their feeling about the action. Just as the expression of a feeling of pain ("Ouch!") is neither true nor false, so also the expression of a feeling about morality ("That's wrong!") is neither true nor false. When we make moral judgments, we do not think, we simply *emote*—hence the name *emotivism*.

The Moralist's Reply to Emotivism

Emotivists argue that scientific claims are objective because they "correspond with reality," while ethical claims are subjective because they do not pretend to correspond with reality. For the moralist, such glorification of science is not logically justifiable. In truth we never know whether *any* scientific claim corresponds with reality, because we never perceive reality as it *is*, only as it *appears* to us. We can never take a position from which we compare our perceptions with reality; we can only compare some of our perceptions with other of our perceptions. It follows that scientific claims are no more objective than moral claims.

Furthermore, even if some scientific claims *could* correspond with reality, it is hardly likely any of our *present* scientific claims do. Science in its modern mathematical form is only several centuries old, and almost every branch of science in this century has undergone a revolution in which the ideas of previous centuries have been thoroughly repudiated. It is hardly likely that, in the twentieth century, science has at last obtained absolute truth, and that scientific revolutions will never again occur. It is likely every scientific theory that we now hold dear will be considered sheer superstition by future generations. Which theory is more likely to be respected in the twenty-fifth century: the current scientific theory that the electron is an elementary atomic particle, or the current moral theory that every adult has the right to vote? The answer is not obvious. But if the answer is not obvious, it is not obvious that scientific theories are more objective than moral theories.

Subjectivists argue that ethical claims lack truth because they are "based on feelings." But the idea that "feelings cannot be justified" is simply mistaken. Normally we distinguish between justified (or appropriate) feelings and unjustified (or inappropriate) feelings. For example, it is appropriate to feel sad at a close relative's funeral; it is inappropriate to feel happy when one has been insulted. But if feelings can be justified *and* moral judgments are tied to feelings, then moral judgments *can* be justified. A justified moral judgment is one based on justified feelings; an unjustified moral judgment is one based on unjustified feelings.

The Idea of a Rationally Justified Ethics

Contrary to determinists, moralists feel ethical judgments are not pointless. Against the relativists, they believe there is a single correct moral code for all the people of the world. Against the emotivists, they believe it is possible to present rational arguments about what this universal code says. But how can we identify this universal moral code? Many moralists answer this question by seeking a rational *foundation* for ethics: a set of facts or truths on which all thoughtful people should agree and from which the rules of a true ethics can be derived.

We will consider three candidates for the foundation of ethics: God, nature, and reason. Perhaps one of these can supply a standard by which one should live one's life.

The Divine Command Theory

The divine command theory of morality maintains that the foundation of ethics is the will of God. On this view, "X is wrong" means "God forbids X"; "X is morally obligatory" means "God commands X." To live well is to live in accordance with the will of God.

Notice the divine command theory does not merely say, *X is wrong* if and only if *God forbids X*. It says that God's commandment *not* to do X is what *makes* it wrong to do X. Likewise, the theory says that God's commandment to *do* Y is what makes it obligatory to do Y. On this theory, whatever God says is right *is* right *because* He says it, and we are all morally obliged to do whatever God says. In the Bible, Abraham seems to have accepted the divine command theory. He felt it was obligatory to slay his innocent son Isaac because God commanded him to do so (Genesis 22:3).

The main argument for the divine command theory is this. A moral rule is a command that tells us what to do. Although these commands do not seem to be created by any human being, they bind all human beings, great and small: it is as morally wrong for a king to commit murder as it is for anyone else. It follows that moral laws must be commands issued by someone higher in authority than any human being. The logical candidate for the source of these commands is God.

Nonreligious persons may object that the divine command theory has one serious flaw: it assumes the existence of God. But this objection is mistaken. The divine command theory does not assume that God exists. It only claims that *if* God exists, His word is the moral law; and *if* God does *not* exist, there are no true moral laws. As the Russian author Fyodor Dostoyevsky wrote in the nineteenth century, if God does not exist, everything is permitted. Thus, surprisingly, the divine command theory can be accepted without contradiction even by atheists.

Criticism of the Divine Command Theory

Like Abraham, many devout people accept the divine command theory. But many philosophers have rejected it—including some who have been devoutly religious. It is important to recognize that belief in God, by itself, does *not* require belief in divine command ethics. God is, by definition, supremely good. It follows from this that He would never *break* the moral law; but it does not follow from this that God *created* the moral law, as the divine command theory claims. The laws of morality might be related to God as the laws of arithmetic are related to God. God, being supremely intelligent, will never break the laws of arithmetic. It does not follow from this, however, that God *created* the law that two plus two makes four.

Here are five arguments against the divine command theory.

1. In practical use, the theory assumes we can know what God commands, or at least that our knowledge of God's commands is more sound than our

knowledge of moral principles. But many people are more confident about right and wrong than they are confident about God's will. In fact, we often make up our minds about what God's will is on the basis of our assumptions about right and wrong. When a mass murderer tells us he was obeying a divine voice that told him to kill, we assume that the man is mad and that he is not hearing *God's* voice. We are confident that mass murder is wrong. From this we conclude that God would not command any individual to commit mass murder. This shows that we *first* make up our minds about right and wrong, and *then* go on to figure out what is the will of God.

2. Suppose God does exist and He has issued a certain command. Either God has a reason for this command or He does not. If He does not, his command is arbitrary and cannot be morally binding. If He does have a reason, then that reason has determined God's choice of commands. He could not, then, have issued a *different* command. But the divine command theory says that God can issue any commands He likes.

3. Normally when we have an obligation, we have done something to acquire the obligation. For example, we acquire an obligation to pay back a loan when we take it out. But the human race does not seem to have done anything by which we acquire obligations to God. Even if God created us, we did not ask to be created. Our creation did not require any work or sacrifice on God's part. And it does not seem that God *needs* to have His commands obeyed. He can get whatever He wants without our help.

4. If the divine command theory is right, then anything God commands is morally obligatory. Thus, if God commands the torture of a baby for purposes of amusement, the torture of that baby would be morally right. But many people believe it would *never* be right, in any circumstances, to torture a baby to death for purposes of amusement. Anyone who believes certain kinds of actions are *intrinsically* wrong must reject the divine command theory.

5. If there is no God, there are no moral laws. It follows that if there is no God, then Hitler did nothing wrong. But for many people, what Hitler did was wrong, God or no God.

Natural Law Ethics

The General Idea of Natural Law.   There are many societies with many different moral codes. But all people are members of the same biological species, and all human societies are located in the same natural world. Because of this, many philosophers have suggested that the foundation for ethics must lie in nature. On this account, a moral act is a natural act, and an immoral act is an unnatural act. Such a view is called *natural law ethics*.

According to natural law ethics, it is foolish to base moral judgments on cultural norms, as ethical relativists suggest. Whole societies and whole cultures can be perverted. But nature as a whole can never be perverse, and the laws of nature form a single consistent moral code. Incidentally, such natural laws will be consistent with the laws of God, since—if there is a God—He is the Creator of Nature. But if there is no God, the natural laws still bind.

For natural law ethics, the main task of moral theory is to distinguish natural acts from perverted acts. In some cases the classification may be difficult. But according to natural law theorists, there are many cases in which nature clearly distinguishes right from wrong. Suicide, for example, is morally wrong because it goes against the universal natural desire for self-preservation. Homosexuality is morally wrong because it goes against the natural use of sex for purposes of reproduction. Grounded on the facts of nature, rules forbidding suicide and homosexuality are rules that all societies should accept, regardless of variations in local customs.

Different Conceptions of What Is Natural. Different philosophers, however, have different conceptions of what "nature" is in detail. Each conception will generate its own code of natural law. The Cynics, in classical Greece, equated "unnatural" with "artificial" and argued that it was a moral mistake for human beings to live in cities, wear woven clothes, or eat cooked food. Social Darwinists, nineteenth-century philosophers interpreting Darwin's doctrine of natural selection as a universal war in which only the "fittest" individuals survived, argued that each person should seek to dominate everyone else, and that sympathy for the victims of domination is unnatural. In the same century, Karl Marx took the struggle of class against class as the natural condition of all precommunist societies, and inferred from this that it was reactionary and unnatural to attempt to mitigate class struggle. In the twentieth century, Nazi moralists have viewed as natural the domination of one race over the rest, and declared that any mixing between races is perverse and unnatural.

This lack of consensus about the characteristics of "nature" is a sore spot for natural law ethics. Nevertheless, some conceptions of nature are more powerful and comprehensive than others. We will consider two of the most powerful conceptions of human nature developed by philosophers—Aristotle's and Kant's—and the systems of ethics Aristotle and Kant developed from their ideas about human nature.

Aristotle's Ethics. For Aristotle, nature is an organized ensemble of kinds of things, each one seeking its own kind of good. Human beings are one kind of thing, and each human being seeks a human good. When we ask what kind of thing a human being is, we find that in essence human beings are *social* animals, living in groups, and *rational* animals, making choices by reason and not always by instinct. A proper human life is one lived in accordance with the social and rational elements of human nature. Thus, a person who lives properly lives in an organized society, treats other people in society fairly, and is prepared to defend society from external threats. Persons who live properly neither suppress their instincts and passions nor give in to them, but instead control them according to their rational judgment of what is truly good. In short a proper human life exhibits the virtues of justice, courage, temperance, and wisdom.

These four virtues are not characteristics that human beings would automatically possess. An isolated human being in the woods would never develop them: they arise from lifelong education and training. But though the virtues are artificial, they are not unnatural. Education is a result of social interaction, and human beings are social animals.

Thus, according to Aristotle, human beings are not automatically just or courageous or temperate, and they are not automatically wise. Unwise persons may choose subhuman goods, submit to passions and lusts, or even elect to live outside society. In these ways they transform themselves into subhuman beasts. A partially wise person may seek human goods in general, but fail to recognize and seek them on particular occasions, falling prey to a self-damaging weakness of will. But with education, every human being can grasp what is natural for human beings, and will seek that natural good, which includes all that human beings should hope for.

Kant's Ethics. For Aristotle, human beings, though rational, are physical beings living in a single physical world. For Kant, each human being lives in two worlds: the physical world of space, time, and matter; and a spiritual world created by the human will, which is not subject to the laws of physics. Free acts of will, according to Kant, are expressions of a person's true self, and the spiritual world, which provides ideals for the will to aim at, is more important than the physical world of plain scientific facts.

Thus, the most important part of human beings is their ability to choose their own goals freely, and the task of morality is to respect this freedom. Kant's most basic rule of morality is: *in all actions, treat persons as ends in themselves, and never as means to an end.* Only in this way can we treat human beings as the free beings they are.

At first sight, it may appear that Kant's rule is impossibly strict. If we ride a bus, we use the bus driver; if we get a haircut, we use the barber. How is it possible to avoid using people as means? The answer lies in the doctrine of the social contract, which Kant adapted from the French philosopher Jean Jacques Rousseau (1712–1778). The key idea of the social contract is that social relations are morally legitimate if and only if people rationally consent to enter into them. ("Rational consent" means consent that is voluntary and informed.) We can use the bus driver and the barber if and only if they have rationally consented to drive the bus and cut our hair. If the essence of human nature is freedom, the essence of immorality is coercion.

Criticism of Natural Law Ethics

All forms of natural law ethics agree that the good and the natural are one and the same. They all assume that nature as a whole cannot be evil, and human beings cannot go morally wrong if they act in human ways. This optimism is challengeable. Ancient religious teachers called Gnostics believed the natural world was the creation of an evil spirit and all natural conduct was evil. From the

Gnostic point of view, moral life requires each person not to accept human nature, but to fight against it. Natural law ethics cannot assume the natural universe is good; it must provide some proof. But it is difficult to see how one could prove nature as a whole is good without appealing to some principle *outside* of nature. To appeal to something outside nature is to go beyond natural law ethics.

Even if we assume nature is good, there are still grave difficulties in determining what is natural and what is not. Natural law theorists consider suicide and homosexuality unnatural. But as far back as the historical record goes, people in considerable numbers have committed suicide and engaged in homosexual acts. Since such conduct is rarely found among other animal species, one might conclude that such acts are specifically human, not specifically inhuman. As David Hume argued, everything that happens is a part of nature, and therefore every act is as natural as every other. But if every act is natural, the rule that we should follow nature is an empty rule.

Criticism of Aristotle's Ethics. For Aristotle, each thing should act according to its kind. But how many kinds of things are there, and how should a thing act if it is a member of more than one kind? For example, human beings form a kind, but there are also different kinds of human beings. Suppose I live in ancient Athens and happen to be a human being, a female, and a slave. How should I be treated? According to Aristotle, there is a difference in kind between men and women, and a difference in kind between free citizens and slaves, who were, in Aristotle's view, "born to take orders." So I should be treated *as* a woman and *as* a slave, not as the moral equal of a free male citizen. It seems noble to say that human beings should be treated as human beings; it seems less noble to say that women should be treated as women and slaves as slaves.

Furthermore, there are difficulties with Aristotle's catalog of virtues. For Aristotle, every virtue is a habit that, when exercised, expresses human nature. Therefore, it cannot harm virtuous individuals and cannot harm the society around them. (A destructive habit would be unnatural.) But courage is a virtue, and courage can produce destructive acts: the acts of the courageous Nazi do harm, and the greater the courage the greater the harm. Justice is a virtue, but just conduct can be self-destructive when it is exploited by the unjust. As for wisdom, Aristotle thought the highest form of wisdom was the contemplation of eternal truths. Such contemplation was good, he argued, because it made people most like the immortal gods. But if this is correct, then the highest ethical task is not to remain human, but to become divine. By the strict standards of natural law ethics, such an aspiration is perverse. It seems the only Aristotelian virtue that produces no harm and stays within human bounds is temperance. But if everyone were temperate, what a bore the world would be!

Criticism of Kant's Ethics. Kant's rule that we should always treat people as ends in themselves is a noble rule, and it will give good guidance on many occasions. But Kant claimed this rule was the basic rule from which *all* obligations could be derived. Does Kant's rule cover every problem in ethics? If a person followed Kant's rule perfectly, would he or she be a perfect human being?

Suppose we saw a man beating a chained dog with a stick. We tell him to stop and he says, "Kant's rule tells me only to respect persons; I have no moral obligations to subhuman animals that lack free will." Is this man morally perfect? Or suppose we saw a man walking along a river bank, near another man drowning in the water. The drowning man calls for help, but the first man walks by. "I did nothing wrong," he says, "because I did not use the drowning man as a means to any of my ends." Is this man morally perfect?

And consider this problem.

Jones is a train switchman, and a runaway train is coming toward his switch. If Jones doesn't throw the switch, the train will plow into the station, killing at least five people. If Jones throws the switch, the train will go onto a siding and hit an automobile, killing two people.

Kant's ethics says it would be wrong to throw the switch, because this would be killing two people *as a means* of saving five, and it is always wrong to use people as means. But wouldn't it be permissible, in these circumstances, to throw the switch?

Basing Ethics on Reason (1): The Golden Rule and the Categorical Imperative

In the search for principles on which to base a universal ethics, many philosophers have suggested that the foundation lies in the principles of logic. Though different societies have different customs, the principles of logic and rationality are the same everywhere. For all such "moral rationalists," *moral conduct is rational conduct.*

Different philosophers, of course, have different conceptions of what rational conduct is. Each conception of rational conduct implies its own moral system. Perhaps the oldest of these systems, suggested by the Chinese sage Confucius, interprets *rational* conduct as *logically consistent* conduct. Applied to ethics, the demand for logically consistent conduct generates a moral principle so famous it is called the Golden Rule: Do unto others as you would have them do unto you.

Confucius and the other early thinkers who proposed the Golden Rule did not give a philosophical argument in its support. But if we ask, "Why is it wrong to do something to people that we would not like to have them do to us?" perhaps the most obvious answer is that such an attitude is inconsistent.

Famous as the Golden Rule is, it has its problems as a guide for conduct. I once saw a burglary in progress and went to call the police. Suppose I had asked myself: "What if I were a burglar? Would I like it if someone called the police and had me arrested?" Obviously not. According to the Golden Rule, then, I should not call the police.

Puzzles like this made many philosophers doubt a demand for logical consistency, by itself, could supply an acceptable guide to conduct. But in the eighteenth century, Immanuel Kant attempted to develop a modern version of the Golden Rule that avoided the difficulties in the version of Confucius.

For Kant, rational conduct requires consistency in the reasons for conduct. Every time we perform an action, we have a reason for the action. Call such a reason R. Logical consistency requires that if I believe R is a good reason for a certain action, then R is a good reason for *anyone else* to perform the same kind of action. Consequently, the supreme test of moral rules is that they be consistent when made universal. Thus, Kant argued that everyone should follow a rule he called the Categorical Imperative: *always act in such a way that we could wish our type of conduct would become a universal law.*

To take one of Kant's own examples, suppose we are considering borrowing money without intending to pay it back. We should ask, "What if *everybody* borrowed money without paying it back?" Obviously, if everybody did that, the system of credit and banking would collapse, and we would not be able to achieve what we hoped to achieve by borrowing money without paying it back. For this reason, Kant argued, it is immoral to borrow money without intending to pay it back.

What is the relationship between the Categorical Imperative and Kant's other rule, which says people should be treated as ends, not means? Kant believed the two principles had the same result. For example, if I borrow money from a friend without intending to pay it back, I use my friend as a means. For Kant, the ethics of human nature and the ethics of reason are one and the same.

Criticism of the Categorical Imperative

Kant's Categorical Imperative avoids some of the difficulties of the Golden Rule, but it has problems of its own. Here are three that have troubled philosophers since Kant's day.

1. *Kant does not supply a reason why the Categorical Imperative should be obeyed.* He argues that to violate the Categorical Imperative is to break the rule of consistency. But we can reasonably ask, "Why can't we break the rule of consistency, when it is in our interest to do so?"

2. *Kant does not tell us which description of an action should be used before the Categorical Imperative should be applied.* Suppose I am considering stealing a loaf of bread to feed my starving family. To apply the Categorical Imperative, should I ask, "What if everybody stole bread?" or should I ask, "What if everyone stole bread when this is the only way to feed their families?" If we apply the Categorical Imperative to the first question, the verdict is that it is immoral to steal bread, because if everyone stole bread no one would bake bread. If we apply the Categorical Imperative to the second question, we get the

verdict that it is not immoral to steal bread, because if only the starving steal bread the bakers could stay in business selling to everyone else.

3. *Kant's principle generates counterintuitive results.* If we consider particular cases, strange judgments stem from the Categorical Imperative. Suppose a boy wants to become a baseball player. If he follows Kant's procedure for determining moral action, he should ask, "What if everyone became a baseball player?" Then we would all starve because there would be no farmers. The conclusion would be that it is immoral to become a baseball player.

Basing Ethics on Reason (2): Ethical Egoism

For Kant, rationality was logical consistency. Many philosophers, however, think logical consistency alone cannot explain what makes a rational act rational. A completely crazy person might be completely consistent, acting according to the logic of his or her delusion. In searching for some account of rationality that went beyond logical consistency, many seventeenth- and eighteenth-century philosophers came to characterize rationality as *efficiency*: the skillful adjustment of means to ends. On this account, a rational act is one that produces the most benefit for the least cost. It was not long before the new conception of rationality-as-efficiency was applied to ethics.

One problem with the conception of rationality-as-efficiency is that it is ambiguous. Is a rational act one that maximizes benefits for *oneself,* or is it one that maximizes benefits for *everyone*? If we say "oneself," we will be led toward an ethical theory called *egoism.* If we say "everyone," we will be led toward an ethical theory called *utilitarianism.* We will consider egoism first.

The basic moral principle of egoism is that *a morally right act is the one that produces the most good for the person who performs it.* For most theories, being self-centered is a vice. Egoism makes it into a virtue. For most theories, persons who sacrifice themselves for others are moral heroes. According to egoism, they are moral fools.

From ancient times, philosophers like Plato have represented the egoist as a sort of madman, living without restraints, incapable of love, bestial, self-indulgent, deceitful, arrogant, and mean. But a person who faithfully follows the egoist code need not be like this. True egoists seek to maximize the good in their entire lives, not just in the short run. Consequently, they will control desires, such as the desire for alcohol, the indulgence of which is ruinous in the long run. Most egoist philosophers preach moderation in food, drink, and sex, and recommend exploration of intellectual pleasures like philosophy and social pleasures like friendship. The Greek egoist Epicurus argued that the truly rational person should live on little besides bread and water, and he recommended this on the egoistic grounds of preserving life and health.

True egoists will not be arrogant and mean, since these attitudes will arouse hostility detrimental to their long-term interests. They generally will be honest, since honesty is usually the best policy. If loving others is a part of the good life, then egoists will not resist the impulse to love others. If kindness and generosity provide special satisfactions, they will be kind and generous in order to obtain those satisfactions. The one thing egoists will not do is *sacrifice* for others. In particular, they will never sacrifice themselves to save anyone else.

Criticism of Ethical Egoism

Egoists interpret rationality-as-efficiency as implying that a rational act is one that maximizes benefits to themselves. But consider an act that is beneficial to the egoist but causes great harm to many others, for example, a stock swindle in which the egoist pockets the cash and everyone else is ruined. By the egoist's definition, this act is a rational act, provided the perpetrator can get away with it. But why should we consider it *rational?* The plain fact is that it does more harm than good, which seems to make it very *inefficient.*

Egoists will reply that the act is bad for others but good for them. They are prejudiced in their own favor and count a dollar as valuable if it is in their pockets and valueless if it is in anyone else's pocket. Is it rational to be so prejudiced in favor of oneself? If one object is more valuable than another, there must be some feature of the object that makes it more valuable. But it hardly makes sense to say a dollar becomes more valuable when it becomes *mine*. If a person says, "I should keep this money because I have done something to deserve it," he has a rational argument. But it is not a rational argument—in fact, it is gibberish—to say, "I should keep the money because I am *me*."

Egoism says each person should seek to maximize his or her personal benefit. This assumes that each person wants to maximize his or her own personal benefit. But it is a plain fact of life that people do not always want to maximize their own personal benefit. If a soldier willingly lays down his life for his country, he is not maximizing his own personal benefit, since he will not be around to collect benefits after he is dead. Nevertheless, he may be doing what he most wants to do at the time. According to egoism, the soldier is irrational. But how can it be irrational to do the thing you most want to do?

Furthermore, the picture of the egoist as an honest law-abiding citizen is quite deceptive. People are *law-abiding* not merely if they obey the law when they're afraid of being caught, but only if they obey the law when they have *no* fear of being caught. By this standard, no egoist is law-abiding. Egoists obey the law only when it maximizes their own good to do so. But if any egoist became suddenly much more powerful, if she discovered, for example, a ring that would make her invisible and her crimes undetectable, then there is no crime that she would not commit so long as it would maximize her good.

Finally, egoism falls into a logical paradox regarding the role of love in human life. Most people agree that those who live their life without loving anyone have missed something very valuable in human existence. But to love someone is to feel her feelings and interests are at least as important as one's own. It follows that no true egoist can love anyone, since no true egoist can concede that someone else's feelings and interests are as important as his own. By making their own good the supreme goal in life, egoists deprive themselves of any chance of experiencing an essential element of that good.

Basing Ethics on Reason (3): Utilitarianism

The egoist says that the right act is the one most profitable for *oneself*. For moralists called *utilitarians,* the right act is the one most profitable for *everyone involved*. But how can we determine the "most profitable act for everyone involved"?

According to the utilitarians, the most profitable act is identified by a five-step procedure.

1. *Imagine* all the alternative actions available;

2. *Predict* as rationally as possible what the consequences of each alternative act will be;

3. *Estimate* the balance of good or bad in the consequences of each act, taking into account every human being and every entity whose welfare is affected by the action;

4. *Compare* the amount of good in the consequences of each alternative action with the amount of good in each of the alternatives;

5. *Select* the act that produces the consequences containing the most good (or least bad) compared with the alternatives.

Notice that to go through step 3 we must have some conception of what "good" and "bad" are. Different utilitarians have different definitions of "good," and these different definitions give rise to many varieties of utilitarianism.

In the eighteenth and nineteenth centuries, most utilitarians were *hedonists,* and they defined "good" as *pleasure and happiness* and "bad" as *pain and misery*. If we plug the hedonistic definition of good into the five-step system described above, the result is the famous formula, first stated in the late eighteenth century by Jeremy Bentham (1748–1832): *the right act is the one that produces the greatest happiness for the greatest number*.

In the twentieth century, most utilitarians have rejected the strict hedonistic definition of "good" and have defined it in terms of a list of *basic goods*. Basic goods include life itself, health, freedom from pain, friendship, aesthetic appreciation, meaningful work, and the freedom to choose one's style of life. But however the utilitarians may disagree on the definition of "good," they all agree on one thing: *the right act is the one that produces the most good*.

When Bentham first stated the utilitarian philosophy, many people were scandalized: they said utilitarianism was not an ethics for people, but an ethics for pigs. The idea that producing happiness is the basic objective of morality angered traditional moralists, who felt the highest human good consists in discharging one's duties, sacrificing heroically for God and country, or contributing to the arts and sciences. But Bentham asked his critics, over and over, what is the good of discharging one's duties, of making sacrifices, of developing the arts and sciences, if these things, in the end, make no contribution to the happiness of human beings? Indeed, what is the reason for doing anything, unless doing it will produce some good, and what is the reason for *not* doing something, unless doing it will produce some harm?

Against the charge that utilitarians never make moral sacrifices, Bentham pointed out that utilitarianism demands as much in the way of sacrifice as any other moral code. According to utilitarianism, an individual must sacrifice his possessions, his time and effort, and even his life, *whenever* the greater good requires it. In fact, once the critics of utilitarianism grasped this point, they shifted from arguing that utilitarianism was a false ethics because it demanded no sacrifices to arguing that utilitarianism was a false ethics because it demanded too many sacrifices.

Other critics of utilitarianism were appalled by the utilitarian idea that *any* act is morally legitimate if it produces more good than any alternative act. This implies that it is morally legitimate to torture babies, if so doing produces the greatest good, or to kill an innocent man, if so doing produces the greatest good. To many, these conclusions are horrible. But the utilitarians are not intimidated by these examples. Suppose the *only* way to prevent *10,000* babies from being tortured were to torture *one* baby, the utilitarians ask, would it not then be right to do so? Suppose the only way to save *10,000* innocent men from death would be to kill *one* innocent man? Would it not then be obligatory to do so? True, we would be very emotionally upset when we did these dreadful acts. But utilitarianism says that ethics should be based on reason, not emotion, and reason says that we should always do what is best on balance.

Criticism of Utilitarianism

The claim of utilitarianism to base ethics on reason has a powerful appeal, and every student of ethics must take some stand, pro or con, regarding the utilitarian system. We will begin with four attacks from people who dislike the results of utilitarian reasoning.

The Rights Objection. Utilitarianism, as we have seen, will occasionally recommend drastic actions, like torturing babies or killing innocent people. Utilitarians justify such acts by appealing to the large positive results: saving 10,000 babies from torture, or saving 10,000 lives. But, in fact, utilitarianism will recommend such horrible acts even when they produce just a *small* balance of good over evil. Utilitarianism says that it is obligatory to torture *five* babies in order to save *six* babies from torture, to kill *five* innocent men in order to save *six.* To many, this seems implausible. Critics of utilitarianism argue that people have a right not to be tortured and a right not to be killed, rights that it is immoral to violate except in the most extreme circumstances.

The Justice Objection. Utilitarianism judges the morality of actions solely according to the amount of good they produce. But morality requires that we consider not only the *amount* of good but the justice of the way this good is *distributed* among persons. For example, World A, in which the wicked are happy and the good are unhappy, is obviously less just than World B, in which the wicked are unhappy and the good are happy, even if the amount of happiness in World A is the same as the amount of happiness in World B. Utilitarianism seems wrong when it says that there is no moral difference between World A and World B. Similarly, a world in which *one* person is very happy when *most* people are miserable seems less just than a world in which everyone is moderately happy, even if the sum total of happiness is the same in both worlds. But utilitarianism maintains that the two worlds are equally desirable if the same total of happiness is present in each.

The Deserts Objection. Utilitarianism judges actions without any reference to past events, but morality requires that past events be considered. For example, if we have made a promise to meet someone, we are bound to keep it, not because of future bad consequences, but because of past commitments. The person to whom we have made the promise *deserves* our good faith. Likewise, if someone commits a crime, he or she *deserves* to be punished because of his or her past crime, even if the punishment will produce no good results.

The Self-Defense Objection. Utilitarianism requires that the life of one individual be considered equal in value to the life of any other. It follows that an individual cannot consider *his or her own* life more important than any other when making decisions in which his or her own life is at stake. Now, suppose I am attacked by five people who wish to kill me, and I have a hidden gun with which I can kill all of them. Utilitarianism says that five lives are more valuable than one and, therefore, it is immoral for me to use the gun. But common sense cries out that individuals have a right to self-defense, which permits them to take steps to save their lives, even if these steps do not produce the greatest total good.

In short, a conscientious utilitarian will violate basic rights, trample over justice, assign rewards and punishments irrespective of merit, and force individuals to ignore their own interests and even their own lives. These are serious objections indeed. But utilitarians have heard them all before and have prepared answers to each. It is not possible here to survey the answers and the answers to these answers, but there are several general points utilitarians make in answer to arguments like these.

First, have all the alternatives been considered? Is it really *necessary* to kill five men to save six? Second, have all the *side effects* been considered? For example, when a promise is broken, it has the bad effect of making people more mistrustful of each other; and this bad effect has to be entered into the utilitarian calculation before permission to break the promise is granted. Third, have the *positive effects of redistribution* been considered? In a society with rich and poor people, one dollar taken from the rich and given to the poor will increase the total good, since a poor person can improve his or her life more with one dollar than a rich person can. In general, utilitarianism favors social equality. Finally, does the objection to utilitarianism rest on anything more than a *mere intuition* about right and wrong (for example, "it is always wrong to break a promise")? If it does, it may be the intuition that is incorrect, not the utilitarian system. After all, many past intuitions about right and wrong have turned out to be unenlightened prejudices.

The reader should consider whether these rebuttals answer objections 1 through 4. Utilitarianism, however, has a deeper problem that it cannot dismiss as prejudice.

The Problem of Interpersonal Comparisons of Good. The utilitarian calculation requires us to add together the goods of different people to determine a *sum total* of good. But can the good of one person be compared to the good of another? Suppose Smith and Brown have headaches and Jones has one (indivisible) aspirin tablet. Jones wants to be a good utilitarian and use the aspirin to produce the most good. How can Jones compare the pain of Smith's headache with the pain of Brown's headache, and how can he measure the quantity of relief the aspirin will provide to each? Smith may say, "My headache is stupendous, agonizing, awful," while Brown just says, "My headache is pretty bad." But this does not prove that Smith's headache is worse. Smith may just be a whining weakling, while Brown keeps a stiff upper lip.

This problem gets even worse when we are comparing different *kinds* of good. Suppose Smith enjoys crowds of people while Brown prefers quiet and empty streets. If a new development is built in town, Smith will be better off and Brown worse off. But how can we tell if the improvement in Smith's life is greater than the decline in Brown's life?

Utilitarians have struggled with this issue and developed tentative answers, none of which has gained common acceptance. But if the good of different individuals cannot be added together, utilitarianism collapses as a moral theory.

Basing Ethics on Reason (4): The Social Contract Theory

Utilitarianism says that we should always sacrifice ourselves for the common good. Egoism says that we should never sacrifice ourselves for anybody. The social contract theory of ethics strikes a balance between these extremes. It says that we should sacrifice for the common good when others in our society are prepared to make the same sacrifice.

Initially, the social contract theory agrees with egoism: each person should always seek to maximize his or her own good. But social contract theorists observe that, in certain situations, the policy of maximizing one's own good can be self-defeating. These are situations, called Prisoner's Dilemmas,[1] in which everyone is worse off if everyone seeks to maximize his or her good.

Consider a crowd of spectators at an exciting football game. Each person wants most of all to see the game perfectly. Secondarily, each person prefers sitting to standing. With this in mind, each person egoistically thinks

1. If the others sit, I should stand, and thereby see perfectly;

2. If the others stand, I should stand, or else my view will be blocked.

Consequently, each person concludes

3. I ought to stand no matter what the others do.

As a result,

4. Everyone stands.

Of course, this is an unfortunate result, since it is better for everyone if everyone sits than if everyone stands. Situations of this type pervade social life. The spectators are caught in a Prisoner's Dilemma, and it is the task of the social contract theory to get them out of it.

Social contract theorists focus attention on step 3. Step 3 exhibits a policy of *unconstrained* maximization: get as much as possible for oneself and forget everyone else. But this reasoning, commonly adopted, leads to step 4, a bad result for everyone. To forestall results like 4, social contract theorists recommend a policy of *constrained* maximization. In this case, constrained maximization implies

3′. I ought to sit *if everyone else sits*; otherwise, I'll stand.

Now, if everyone acts according to step 3′, everyone sits and everyone sees the game.

What has all this to do with morality? According to social contract theory, moral rules are simply rules for escaping Prisoner's Dilemmas: *moral conduct is simply constrained maximization.*

Notice that constrained maximization—or cooperation—requires a sacrifice. In the football example, there are four possible outcomes:

1. I stand, everyone else sits. (Best)

2. Everyone sits. (Second best)

3. Everyone stands. (Third best)

4. I sit; everyone else stands. (Worst)

If I choose cooperation, I sacrifice all hope of obtaining my best outcome, 1. But this is a sacrifice I make only on the condition that everyone else makes the same sacrifice. It is rational to be a constrained maximizer only in a society

---

[1] For an explanation of this label, see Suggestions for Further Reading, page 112.

of constrained maximizers. The social contract is an implicit agreement among constrained maximizers that each will continue to restrain him- or herself so long as the others do. Such conduct is not egoistic, but it is not irrational. Each constrained maximizer loses the best outcome. But each is rewarded with the second-best outcome, and each avoids both 3 and 4.

Suppose I am willing to restrain myself if others do. But the people around me are pure egoists, unconstrained maximizers. Am I morally obliged to restrain myself? Not at all. In the social contract theory, moral conduct is always rational conduct, never pure sacrifice. Surrounded by egoists, each person has no choice but to be an egoist. But persons who are prepared to restrain themselves if others do, hope that others will be persuaded to cooperate. Even as egoists, they will seek to create the conditions of mutual trust, which make cooperation possible.

Criticism of the Social Contract Theory

The social contract theory of ethics is under intense discussion in contemporary philosophy. Many are persuaded that this theory, more than any other, shows the proper relation between moral conduct and rational conduct. Many are unpersuaded. Here are two arguments from the nonbelievers.

1. In the social contract theory, moral relationships exist between members of a community of cooperating people, each of whom has made a sacrifice for the common good. But what about individuals who cannot make sacrifices? The social contract theory says that they are not members of the community and have no moral rights. This is hard to believe.

Suppose, at the football game, almost everyone in Jones's seat section is disabled and confined to wheelchairs. Jones takes advantage of the situation and stands up. This gives him a perfect view of the game, but blocks the view of the handicapped people behind him. According to the social contract theory, there is no reason for Jones to sit down. He need not worry, if he stands up, that the others will stand up, because they *can't* stand up. So Jones has no reason to give up his best outcome in order to avoid his third-best outcome. But whatever the social contract theory says, it does seem wrong for Jones to take advantage of the handicapped people. The decent thing for Jones to do is sit down, even if, by social contract standards, this is not the rational thing to do.

The social contract theory defines moral relations between individuals of roughly equal strength. It denies the existence of moral relations between parties of unequal strength. But many of the most important moral relationships—between parents and children, between adults and their elderly parents, between the handicapped and nonhandicapped, between human beings and nonhuman animals—are between parties of unequal strength. The same is true of relationships between ordinary people and helpless strangers.

Suppose we're driving down the road and see a man lying on the road, hurt in an automobile accident. We have a moral obligation to help: not because we expect that someday this person—or any person—will help us. We have an obligation to help because he *needs* help. The basis of morality is simply human need, not anything so fancy as "a contract to constrain maximization in a Prisoner's Dilemma."

2. Suppose the football game is tied with three seconds to go. Time is called, and the home team prepares to kick a field goal, which will bring victory if successful. Jones is sitting with his fellow cooperators, who remain seated. Just as the ball is kicked, Jones jumps up and gets a perfect view of the final play. Of course, his act blocks the view of the people behind him. Has Jones acted irrationally? Certainly not: he got what he wanted; and since the game is over, no one is going to jump up and block *his* view. Since the act is rational, the social contract theory cannot condemn it. Nevertheless, Jones has given up cooperating, and has taken advantage of the cooperative attitude of the people who remain seated.

The problem here is that there is no need for Jones to go on sitting, so long as he is confident the others will continue to sit. In general, cooperators have no reason to go on cooperating, so long as they have reason to believe everyone else will continue to cooperate. The social contract theory has failed to demonstrate its basic premise: *it is rational to cooperate with cooperative people.*

Ethics Without Foundations

In the preceding sections, we have considered three different theories about the foundations of ethics. Each of these theories, however, has been subjected to severe criticism. Suppose every such attempt to find a foundation for ethics fails. Must we abandon all hope for an objective universal ethics, and fall back into relativism or emotivism? Not necessarily. Perhaps ethical claims can be justified without reference to foundations.

In traditional geometry we begin with general claims that are called "self-evident." From these claims, we proceed, using logic, to prove claims that are not self-evident. To do ethics in similar fashion, we might start with self-evident general moral claims. One such claim might be that it's always wrong to torture a baby for fun. From these self-evident claims we could then proceed to prove other moral truths.

Finally, suppose people cannot agree on any self-evident general truths in ethics, not even about torturing babies. We still have our feelings of right and wrong about specific cases. Starting with these feelings, we can then apply the *rule of moral consistency*:

If two cases are similar in relevant respects, then we should have the same moral feeling about both.

With this rule, we can form moral judgments about cases where we originally had no moral feelings. We might also discover that some of our moral feelings are inconsistent with each other. In such cases, we should adjust our feelings to restore consistency. As a moral theory, this might not seem like much. But the rule of moral consistency can be a powerful tool in ethics. We will see it at work in our discussion of abortion.

The Moral Case Against Abortion

The purpose of ethics is to guide conduct. Let us consider what the moral theories presented here say about one of the most controversial moral issues of our time: the morality of induced abortion.

Induced abortions take place in a wide variety of circumstances, and a good deal of discussion about abortion is taken up with special cases: Is abortion permissible when the abortion is necessary for the mother's health? When the fetus is defective? When the pregnancy results from rape? When the pregnancy is well advanced? and so forth. The special cases, however, concern only a small fraction of the 1.3 million abortions performed in the United States every year. Let us concentrate on the *typical* abortion: an abortion performed in the first three months of pregnancy, when the pregnancy does not result from rape, when the fetus is not known to be defective, and when the pregnancy is not dangerous to the mother's physical health. Is the act of abortion morally wrong in *these* circumstances? The Catholic Church, many Protestant sects, and millions of Americans think it is. The following argument is a summary of their case.

A human life, abortion opponents argue, begins with conception. At conception the DNA that contains the instructions for constructing a complete and unique human being is assembled. The odds that a human being with such a genetic pattern will ever be born are negligible before conception but substantial after conception. The zygote that results from conception is a living human organism that will, in the natural and continuous course of events, develop into a fetus, a baby, a child, an adolescent, and an adult human being. These are all stages of one single human life, and a zygote is therefore just as much a human being as a baby or an adult. The Bible itself recognizes that human life begins before birth. As God said to Jeremiah: "Before I formed thee in the belly, I knew ye; before thou camest out of the womb, I sanctified thee" (Jeremiah 1:5).

Abortion, therefore, is the deliberate taking of a human life. It violates the divine law "thou shalt not kill." It violates the natural law that members of the same species should not kill each other, and it violates the natural obligation that each mother has to protect her own child. It offends against the Golden Rule, since those who request abortions surely would not like to have them performed on themselves; and it violates social contract ethics, since under the social contract we agree not to kill those who do not try to kill us. Furthermore, the general acceptance of abortion has bad social consequences, which should worry utilitarians. Once one class of undesirable human beings is singled out for killing, it becomes more probable that other classes will be singled out. The next step is another Holocaust.

There are certain cases in which it is legitimate to take human life; for example, executing murderers or self-defense. But the fetus is entirely innocent;

and, in a typical abortion, the fetus is no threat to its mother's life. The typical abortion, then, is murder, and murder of a particularly despicable kind, since the victim is completely defenseless. Since abortion is murder, it ought to be made illegal, since all societies at all periods of history have considered murder a great crime.

Criticism of the Case Against Abortion

One crucial step in this argument is that a human life begins at conception. But this view is mistaken. Conception produces a one-celled zygote that reproduces (after several hours) by dividing in half; then those halves divide in half, and so forth, producing a colony of semi-independent cells. Now, when any cell, any organism of any kind, reproduces by dividing in half, the original organism *disappears,* and what results is the next generation of cells. The zygote after conception does *not* develop into an embryo the way a child develops into an adult. Instead, it *dies,* and a new generation of cells takes its place. Thus, there is no continuous development from zygote to adult.

When we consider the human fetus at the stage of a typical abortion, we are not dealing with anything like a human person or a human being. The typical aborted fetus has a very rudimentary brain and nervous system. It has no thoughts, no feelings, no mental life. Suppose we could remove such a fetus from its mother's womb and keep it alive indefinitely, *at this level of development.* Would we consider this entity, which is totally incapable of consciousness, which never had and never will have a single thought or feeling, a human person?

Suppose we heard of a person who has suffered massive brain damage in a car accident, and who will live out the rest of his or her days without ever achieving any consciousness, not even a dream. Is this entity a person? In the case of the brain-damaged adult, we have a living thing made of human cells, but nothing that is experiencing a human life. Thus, it is not ending a human life to pull the plug on the brain-damaged accident victim. His or her life has *already* ended, before the plug is pulled. But the brain of a typical aborted fetus has no more consciousness than the brain-damaged accident victim. Thus, the typical abortion cannot be the ending of a human life. A human life has not yet begun.

Opponents of abortion may argue that the fetus is a human person because it has the *potential* to be born, develop consciousness, and become an adult. But at best this shows that a three-month-old fetus is a potential human person, not an actual human person; and a potential person is not a kind of person, no more than a potential lottery winner is a kind of lottery winner.

There is a further problem with the argument that fetuses are people because of their potential. Every cell in the human body (excluding sperm and egg cells, which contain only half the genetic code) contains the full genetic code, and so every cell in the human body contains a blueprint of a human being. By a biological procedure called "cloning," it is theoretically possible to produce a human being from any one of trillions of cells. Every cell in Jones's body is a potential person; indeed, every cell in Jones's body is as much a potential person as a fertilized human egg is a potential person. If it is murder to kill potential people, then murder is committed every time Jones goes to the barber, since the barber kills some of Jones's cells.

Abortion, then, is not the taking of a human life and is not forbidden by the biblical rule "thou shalt not kill." In fact, the Bible nowhere forbids abortion, and Mosaic law (Exodus 21:22) does not classify an induced miscarriage as an act of homicide. The passage from Jeremiah, quoted earlier, implies not that Jeremiah existed in the womb, but that God foresaw the coming of Jeremiah ages before his birth.

Abortion does not violate the natural behavior of human beings toward each other, because there is no "other," nor does it violate the natural behavior of a mother toward her child, because there is no child. Abortion does not violate the Golden Rule: no person can fear being aborted in the womb, since, in fact, there is no person in the womb. Furthermore, the social consequences of forbidding abortion are terrible. In the real world, in which adoption is never a panacea, banning abortion results in the birth of thousands of unwanted children to unprepared or overburdened mothers. The happiness of these mothers, and society at large, would be immeasurably increased if they had their children when they want them and when they are better prepared to care for them. Finally, even if the private act of abortion *were* immoral, it would be wrong to make it against the law, since every law that bans abortion is a law that unjustly discriminates against women, placing a burden on the mother and no burden on the father. This violates the social contract that assigns men and women each a fair share of the burdens of life.

The Moral Case for Freedom of Choice

In the section, "Ethics Without Foundations," it was suggested that one way to reach ethical judgments is through feelings about concrete cases, combined with the principle of consistency. To use this approach in the abortion controversy, we need a case, relevantly similar to abortion, about which we have a moral intuition, which we then extend to the abortion case. The example should be one that contains as few controversial assumptions as possible.

The Example. People who get leukemia sometimes can be saved by chemotherapy. If chemotherapy fails, the patient can sometimes be saved by a bone marrow transplant. The marrow from the donor must match the marrow of the patient, and it sometimes happens that the right marrow match involves people who are complete strangers to each other. One day, Jones receives the following letter from a leukemia patient:

Dear Mr. Jones,

You don't know me, but I am a leukemia patient who will soon die unless I receive a bone marrow transplant. The computers have identified you as the only suitable donor. If you agree, you must donate the marrow in four surgical operations, each one month apart. Please save me!

Hopefully,
John Smith

Jones writes in return:

Dear Mr. Smith,

It's not often one gets a chance to save a fellow human being. I will try to help you and will begin the series of operations, though I'm not sure I can do them all.

Sincerely,
Bill Jones

Jones goes through the first two operations, but finds the surgery extremely unpleasant. He wants to stop. Is it morally permissible for him to quit?

Notice that the relationship between Jones and Smith is very much like the relationship between the mother and the fetus. Jones is the only person who can keep Smith alive; the mother is the only person who can keep the fetus alive. If the mother had not become pregnant, the fetus would not exist. If Jones had not undertaken the first two operations, Smith would not now exist.

Smith hears about Jones's desire to quit and sends this plea:

Dear Bill,

If you hadn't done what you did, I wouldn't even exist right now. So my life is your responsibility, and you must do what's necessary to keep me alive. If you stop the operations, you will be deliberately ending my life, and that would be little different from murder.

Apprehensively,
John Smith

But Jones is adamant, and replies:

Dear John,

If I went through with all four operations, that would be a saintly act. But I'm not a saint, and no one is morally required to be a saint. It's true that, if I hadn't started these operations, you would not now exist. But this shows only that I have been your benefactor, not that I am responsible for you and now owe you anything. How can I, your benefactor, be indebted to you?

The fact is that you have no right to my bone marrow or to my help. My bone marrow is a part of me, and no one has a moral right to use me without my permission, and permission is something that must be given freely: it cannot be required. In this case, sadly, I refuse.

Regretfully,
Bill Jones

Many will agree that Jones does not have a moral duty to undergo two further bone marrow transplant operations. The justification is found in Kant's rule: no person has the right to use another as a means, without permission. But, *if* Jones has no duty to give the marrow, no mother has a duty to continue a pregnancy, even if we assume the fetus is a human person. The fetus uses the mother's body to survive, just as Smith uses the marrow from Jones to survive. The two situations are relevantly similar. Whatever moral judgment one makes about the bone marrow case, the rule of consistency requires the same judgment about the pregnancy case.

Criticism of The Case for Freedom of Choice

To begin, it is not obvious to everyone that Jones has a moral right to refuse Smith's request. For those who think Jones has a duty to give the marrow, this defense of abortion fails completely.

Furthermore, there are significant differences between the bone marrow case and the pregnancy case. Smith is a complete stranger to Jones, while the fetus is biologically related to its mother. And there is a significant difference between the *refusal of marrow* and the *act of abortion*. The refusal of marrow involves only inactivity; abortion requires violence directed against a living thing. If Jones refuses marrow, *leukemia* will kill Smith. When the mother has an abortion, the *doctor* will kill the fetus, at her request. Would it be morally permissible for Jones to bash Smith's head in with a rock, if this were the only way to prevent Smith from getting more marrow?

Jones justifies his refusal on the grounds that Smith has no right to use his body without permission. Isn't it strange to think of pregnancy in these terms? Is a fetus really using its mother as a means? A fetus has no goals that it forces its mother to serve. It is not *using* its mother, since it is not *doing* anything. It is merely living, and to go on living is its natural right.

Final Reflections on Ethics and Abortion

On balance, natural law ethics of the Aristotelian sort tends to condemn abortion. Natural law ethics of the Kantian sort and utilitarianism, with some qualifications, favor freedom of choice. So does ethical egoism.

If we believe the Pope is an infallible authority on the word of God, we will believe that divine command ethics condemns abortion. If we believe the Bible is the prime source of knowledge about God's word, we will believe that divine command ethics is silent on the abortion issue.

If we believe the fetus is *not* a person, then social contract ethics and the Golden Rule favor freedom of choice. If we believe that the fetus *is* a person, then social contract ethics and the Golden Rule will condemn abortion.

In view of all this disagreement, one is tempted to throw up one's hands and say that ethical theories are useless as guides to life. The theories are hopelessly deadlocked, and some of the most important issues—for example, the issue of whether or not a fetus is a person—seem to lie outside ethics altogether. Wouldn't it be better to operate with a "gut feeling" about the morality of abortion, rather than leaving this problem to a moral theory?

Most philosophers caution that recourse to gut feelings is a bad idea. In the past, people have had gut feelings that have been absolutely convincing and absolutely mistaken. Consider, for example, the gut feeling, common in parts of this country before 1865, that slavery was morally permissible. In the end, a feeling backed by a rational argument is more likely to be true than a feeling backed by instinct.

In the case of abortion, philosophical theories disagree and scientific issues intrude. Nevertheless, the theories on one or the other side of the abortion issue may eventually be vindicated. Finally, logic provides one rock-bottom check on both theories and gut feelings. Whatever we believe about abortion, it should be logically consistent with everything else we believe about what is right and what is good. Whether discussing ethics, immortality, or the existence of God, consistency is the primary requirement of the philosophical life.

SUGGESTIONS FOR FURTHER READING

Scepticism About Ethics
Students interested in the history of ethics should consult Henry Sidgwick, *Outlines of the History of Ethics* [1886] (Boston: Beacon Press, 1964) and Alasdair Macintyre, *A Short History of Ethics* (New York: Macmillan, 1966).

Plato's views about ethics are contained in discussions called "Dialogues." The most important ethical discussions in Plato are in his *Euthyphro, Apology, Crito, Gorgias, Theatetus,* and *Republic.*

First Challenge to Ethics: Determinism
Kant's principle is stated in "Methodology of Pure Practical Reason,"* *Critique of Practical Reason* [1788] (Indianapolis, Ind.: Bobbs-Merrill, 1956 pg. 163).

Two very thorough defenses of the determinism described here were developed in the seventeenth century by Thomas Hobbes (*Of Body*, 1640) and Benedict Spinoza (*Ethics*, 1676). For modern discussions of these issues, see Bernard Berofsky, ed., *Free Will and Determinism** (New York: Harper and Row, 1966); Keith Lehrer, ed., *Freedom and Determinism** (New York: Random House, 1966); and Gary Watson, ed., *Free Will* (Oxford: Oxford University Press, 1975). A very thorough modern defense is Ted Honderich, *A Theory of Determinism** (New York: Oxford University Press, 1988).

---

* Asterisk denotes an advanced technical discussion.

The Moralist's Reply to Determinism

Is Kant's Principle True? The examples given here are adapted from Harry Frankfurt, "Alternative Possibilities and Moral Responsibility,"* *Journal of Philosophy* (1969). For counterarguments that moral responsibility *does* require free will, see Peter Van Inwagen, *An Essay on Free Will** (New York: Oxford University Press, 1983).

Aristotle's discussion of moral responsibility is in his *Nichomachean Ethics*, Book III. (The quotation about "overstraining human nature" is at 1110a10.) For analysis, see Richard Sorabji, *Necessity, Cause, and Blame: Perspectives on Aristotle's Theory* (Ithaca, N.Y.: Cornell University Press, 1980). For modern discussions of responsibility, see Jonathan Glover, *Responsibility* (New York: Humanities Press, 1970); John Martin Fischer, ed., *Moral Responsibility* (Ithaca, N.Y.: Cornell University Press, 1986); and Joel Feinberg, *Doing and Deserving* (Princeton, N.J.: Princeton University Press, 1973).

Is Determinism True? For analysis of "everyone does what he most desires to do," see Derek Parfit, *Reasons and Persons** (New York: Oxford University Press, 1984, Part II). Two spirited attacks on determinism are Karl Popper, *The Open Universe* (Totowa, N.J.: Rowman and Littlefield, 1980), and K. W. Rankin, *Choice and Chance* (Oxford: Basil Blackwell, 1961).

Second Challenge to Ethics: Ethical Relativism

The classic defense of ethical relativism is E. O. Westermarck, *Ethical Relativity* (London: Routledge and Kegan Paul, 1932). For modern defenses of ethical relativism, see Gilbert Harman, *The Nature of Morality* (Oxford: Oxford University Press, 1971); Bernard Williams, *Ethics and the Limits of Philosophy** (Cambridge, Mass.: Harvard University Press, 1985); and Paul Feyerabend, *Farewell to Reason* (London: Verso, 1987).

The Moralist's Reply to Ethical Relativism

There are innumerable replies by moralists to relativism. Perhaps the earliest is Plato's *Theatetus*. One very clear modern one is James Rachels, *The Elements of Moral Philosophy* (New York: Random House, 1986, Ch. 2).

Third Challenge to Ethics: Emotivism

One classic argument for the subjectivity of ethical judgments is David Hume, "The Sceptic," in E. F. Miller, ed., *Essays: Moral, Political, and Literary* [1753] (Indianapolis, Ind.: Liberty Classics, 1987). (But see Hume's qualifications in "On the Standard of Taste" in the same collection of essays.) The classic modern defense of emotivism proper is A. J. Ayer, *Language, Truth and Logic* [1936] (New York: Dover Publications, 1952). C. L. Stevenson, *Ethics and Language* (New Haven, Conn.: Yale University Press, 1944), develops a related theory.

The Moralist's Reply to Emotivism

For the alliance between ethical subjectivism and scientific objectivism, see Jack W. Meiland and Michael Krausz, eds., *Relativism: Cognitive and Moral* (Notre Dame, Ind.: University of Notre Dame Press, 1982).

The idea that restraining the claims of science can make an objective ethics possible is a major theme of Immanuel Kant's *Critique of Pure Reason;* see the Preface to the second edition [1787]. For other arguments for ethical objectivism or "realism," see David Copp and David Zimmerman, eds., *Morality, Reason, and Truth* (Totowa, N.J.: Rowman and Littlefield, 1985), and David McNaughton, *Moral Vision* (Oxford: Basil Blackwell, 1988).

The argument that feelings can be rationally justified is developed in J. N. Findlay, "The Justification of Attitudes," in J. N. Findlay, *Language, Mind, and Value* (London: Allen and Unwin, 1963).

The Idea of a Rationally Justified Ethics

For the argument that ethics must have a rational foundation or collapse into a mishmash of prejudices, see Alan Gewirth, *Reason and Morality** (Chicago: University of Chicago Press, 1978).

The Divine Command Theory

For historical background on divine command ethics, see Janine Marie Idziak, Divine Command Morality: Historical and Contemporary Perspectives (Lewisburg, N.Y.: Mellen, 1980). Modern versions of the divine command theory are defended by Philip Quinn, "Religious Obedience and Moral Autonomy," *Religious Studies* [1975], and by Robert Merrihew Adams, "A Modified Divine Command Theory of Ethical Wrongfulness" [1973], in Paul Helm, ed., *Divine Commands and Moral Requirements* (Oxford: Oxford University Press, 1977).

Criticism of the Divine Command Theory

One classic criticism of a version of the divine command theory is in Plato's *Euthyphro*. A development of this argument is urged, with gusto, by Anthony Flew, *God and Philosophy* (New York: Dell, 1966). See also, Thomas Aquinas, *Summa Theologica** IaIIae Q. 91, 93, 94.

Natural Law Ethics

For the ancient Cynics, see "Cynics," in Paul Edwards, ed., *The Encyclopedia of Philosophy* (New York: Macmillan, 1967). For Social Darwinism, see Herbert Spencer, *Principles of Ethics* [1879–93] (Indianapolis, Ind.: Liberty Classics, 1980). For Marx's ethics, start with *The Communist Manifesto* [1848]. For Nazi ethics, see Adolph Hitler, *Mein Kampf*, Ralph Mannheim, trans. (Boston: Houghton Mifflin, 1943); and Heinrich Himmler's speech to the S.S. commandants [1943], in L. Davidowicz, ed., *The Holocaust Reader* (New York: Behrman House, 1976).

Aristotle's ethics is in two books: *The Nichomachean Ethics* and the *Eudemian Ethics*. Kant's ethics is in four books: *Lectures on Ethics* [1780], *Founda-*

tions of the Metaphysics of Morals [1785], *Critique of Practical Reason** [1788], and *Metaphysics of Morals** [1797]. The degree to which Kant's views are influenced by the notion of a "spiritual world" is analyzed by C. D. Broad, "Immanuel Kant and Psychical Research," in C. Broad, *Religion, Philosophy, and Psychical Research* (London: Routledge and Kegan Paul, 1951), and J. N. Findlay, *Kant and the Transcendental Object* (Oxford: Clarendon Press, 1981).

The reader should note that the classification of Kant as a kind of "natural law" theorist is not commonly accepted by contemporary philosophers.

Criticism of Natural Law Ethics

For Gnosticism, see Hans Jonas, *The Gnostic Religion* (Boston: Beacon Press, 1963), and Elaine Pagels, *The Gnostic Gospels* (New York: Random House, 1979).

Hume's criticisms of natural law ethics are in his essay, "Of Suicide," in *Essays: Moral, Political, and Literary.*

Criticism of Aristotle's Ethics.

The problems basing ethics on any theory of virtue are developed in John Hospers, *Human Conduct* (New York: Harcourt Brace, 1961), and Philippa Foot, *Virtues and Vices* (Berkeley: University of California Press, 1978).

Criticism of Kant's Ethics.

Kant's views that animals have no rights is stated in *Lectures on Ethics*, Louis Infield, trans. (New York: Harper and Row, 1963, pp. 239–241); his faltering discussion of charity is on pp. 235–36.

The problem of the train switchman seems to have been introduced into modern ethics in Philippa Foot, "The Problem of Abortion and the Principle of Double Effect," *Oxford Review* (1967), reprinted in *Virtues and Vices.*

Basing Ethics on Reason (1): The Golden Rule and the Categorical Imperative

Kant's clearest presentation of the idea of the Categorical Imperative is in *Foundations of the Metaphysics of Morals* [1785], Louis White Beck, trans. (Indianapolis, Ind.: Bobbs-Merrill, 1959). A modern example of a moral system based on the Categorical Imperative is Onora Nell, *Acting on Principle* (New York: Columbia University Press, 1975).

For a history of the Golden Rule, consult H. O. Westermarck, *Origin and Development of the Moral Ideas* [1906] (Freeport, N.Y.: Books for Libraries, 1971).

Criticism of the Categorical Imperative

One clear critique of the Categorical Imperative is Bernard Gert, *The Moral Rules* (New York: Harper and Row, 1966).

Basing Ethics on Reason: Ethical Egoism

For the development of rationality-as-efficiency, see Joseph Schumpeter, *History of Economic Analysis* (New York: Oxford University Press, 1954), and A. O. Hirschmann, *The Passions and the Interests* (Princeton, N.J.: Princeton University

Press, 1974). The first to apply cost-benefit analysis to ethics seems to have been Francis Hutcheson, *Inquiry into the Original of our Ideas of Beauty and Virtue* [1725], Part II, reprinted in L. A. Selby-Bigge, *British Moralists* (New York: Dover, 1958).

Two nineteenth-century defenses of ethical egoism are Max Stirner, *The Ego and Its Own* [1845] (New York: 1907), and Friedrich Nietzsche, *Beyond Good and Evil* [1886]. A popular twentieth-century egoist is Ayn Rand, *The Virtue of Selfishness* (New York: Signet Books, 1964).

The caricature of the egoist as unrestrained glutton begins with the description of the egoist Callicles in Plato's *Gorgias*.

Criticism of Ethical Egoism

The argument that rationality consists simply in maximizing good over bad, not *my* good over *my* bad, comes from G. E. Moore, *Principia Ethica** (Cambridge, Eng.: Cambridge University Press, 1903).

For a discussion of rationality-as-self-interest versus rationality-as-desire-satisfaction, see Derek Parfit, *Reasons and Persons* (New York: Oxford University Press, 1985), Ch. 6.

The example of the ring that makes the egoist all-powerful originates in Plato's *Republic*, Book II.

The paradox of love discussed here is similar to many paradoxes discussed by Jon Elster, *Ulysses and the Sirens* (New York: Cambridge University Press, 1979).

Basing Ethics on Reason: Utilitarianism

Classic works of hedonistic utilitarianism include Francis Hutcheson, *Inquiry into the Original of Our Ideas of Beauty and Virtue* [1725]; David Hume, *Enquiry Concerning the Principles of Morals* [1751]; Jeremy Bentham, *Introduction to the Principles of Morals and of Legislation* [1789]; William Godwin, *Enquiry Concerning Political Justice* [1793]; John Stuart Mill, *Utilitarianism* [1863]; and Henry Sidgwick, *The Methods of Ethics* [1874]. A modern defense of hedonistic utilitarianism is T. L. S. Sprigge, *The Rational Foundations of Ethics* (London: Routledge and Kegan Paul, 1988). For nonhedonistic or "ideal" utilitarianism, see G. E. Moore, *Principia Ethica** [1903], and Bertrand Russell, "The Elements of Ethics," in B. Russell, *Philosophical Essays* (London: Longmans, Green, 1910).

Criticism of Utilitarianism

The most vivid set of arguments directed against utilitarianism are given in David Ross, *The Right and the Good* (Oxford: Oxford University Press, 1930). For more technical criticisms, see David Lyons, *Forms and Limits of Utilitarianism** (Oxford: Oxford University Press, 1967); D. H. Hodgson, *Consequences of Utilitarianism** (Oxford: Oxford University Press, 1967); and Shelly Kagan, *The Limits of Morality** (Oxford: Oxford University Press, 1989).

For the problem of interpersonal comparisons of utility and some ways around it, see D. Luce and H. Raiffa, *Games and Decisions* (New York: John Wiley, 1957).

Basing Ethics in Reason (4): The Social Contract Theory

The name "Prisoner's Dilemma" was coined by Princeton mathematician A. W. Tucker, who outlined the problem with the following tale. Two prisoners are held in solitary confinement. The district attorney has enough evidence to convict each of a minor crime (two years in jail), but can convict both of major crimes (ten years in jail) if they both confess. He approaches each prisoner separately with the following plea bargain: "If you confess and the other doesn't, I'll throw the book at him and he'll get twenty years, and you'll get probation. If you don't confess and the other does, I'll throw the book at you; you'll get twenty years, and he'll get probation." Both prisoners confess. Both would have been better off if they had refused to confess. The reader should verify that the structure of this situation is the same as the situation of the spectators at the football game described in this section.

For examples of the Prisoner's Dilemma in a wide variety of settings, see Edna Ullmann-Margalit, *The Emergence of Norms* (Oxford: Oxford University Press, 1977) and Russell Hardin, *Collective Action* (Baltimore, Md.: Johns Hopkins University Press, 1982).

The idea that morality is constrained maximization is developed in David Gauthier, *Morals by Agreement** (New York: Oxford University Press, 1986). Gauthier's theory is discussed by eight philosophers in *Social Philosophy and Policy* (Spring 1988). For other contemporary social contract theories, see Gilbert Harman, *The Nature of Morality* (New York: Oxford University Press, 1976).

Criticism of the Social Contract Theory

For criticisms of social contract theories of the Gauthier sort, see Virginia Held, "The Grounds for Social Trust," in V. Held, *Rights and Goods* (New York: Free Press, 1984); Robert Goodin, *Protecting the Vulnerable* (Chicago: University of Chicago Press, 1985); Annette Baier, "The Need for More Than Justice," *Canadian Journal of Philosophy*, supplementary volume on science, morality, and feminist theory (1987); and Annette Baier, "Pilgrim's Progress," *Canadian Journal of Philosophy* (June 1988).

Ethics Without Foundations

A classic argument against the attempt to provide a rational foundation for ethics is H. A. Prichard, "Does Moral Philosophy Rest on Mistake?" [1912], in H. Prichard, *Moral Obligation* (Oxford: Clarendon Press, 1949). See also, Alasdair MacIntyre, *After Virtue* (Notre Dame, Ind.: University of Notre Dame Press, 1982).

The Moral Case Against Abortion

The case against abortion given here is assembled from many sources, including Germain C. Grisez, *Abortion: The Myths, Realities, and the Arguments* (Washington, D.C.: Corpus Books, 1969); John T. Noonan, Jr., ed., *The Morality of Abortion: Legal and Historical Perspectives* (Cambridge, Mass.: Harvard University Press, 1970); John Garvey and Frank Morris, eds., *Abortion: Catholic Perspectives* (Chicago: Thomas More Press, 1979); and Thomas W. Hilgers, Dennis J. Horan, and David Mall, eds., *New Perspectives on Human Abortion* (Frederick, Md.: Aletheia Press, 1981).

Criticism of the Case Against Abortion

A good summary of the facts of human gestation as they relate to abortion questions is Clifford Grobstein, "Rights in the Womb," *The Sciences* (April 1982). For discussion of how the Catholic Church came to analyze pregnancy differently, see John R. Connery, *Abortion: The Development of the Roman Catholic Perspective* (Chicago: Loyola University Press, 1977). For analysis of actual versus potential human life, see Joel Feinberg, "Potentiality, Development, and Rights," in J. Feinberg, ed., *The Problem of Abortion* (Belmont, Calif: Wadsworth, 1984).

For an analysis of the biblical materials regarding abortion, see David M. Feldman, *Marital Relations, Birth Control, and Abortion in Jewish Law* (New York: Schocken, 1975). For an analysis of the Golden Rule and abortion, see George Sher, "Hare, Abortion, and the Golden Rule," *Philosophy and Public Affairs* (1977). For the social effects of unwanted children, see Carl Reitman, ed., *Abortion and the Unwanted Child* (New York: Springer, 1971). For a review of materials showing that anti-abortion arguments involve discriminatory attitudes toward women, see Beverly Wildung Harrison, *Our Right to Choose* (Boston: Beacon Press, 1983).

The Moral Case for Freedom of Choice

The bone marrow example is a logical descendant of the famous violinist example set forth in Judith Jarvis Thomson, "A Defense of Abortion" [1971], in Joel Feinberg, ed., *The Problem of Abortion*.

Criticism of the Case for Freedom of Choice

For criticism of the analogy between cases like the bone marrow case and pregnancy, see John Finnis, "The Rights and Wrongs of Abortion: A Reply to Professor Thomson," *Philosophy and Public Affairs* [1973].

For criticism of the argument that if Jones refuses marrow *leukemia* kills Smith in a way that exonerates Jones, see James Rachels, *The End of Life* (New York: Oxford University Press, 1986), pp. 114–116.

Postscript

In this book, we have considered dozens of arguments about God, immortality, and ethics. If these discussions have helped you reach conclusions about these issues, well and good. But aside from specific conclusions about specific issues, is there anything to be learned from these arguments?

One obvious moral is that these issues are more complicated than they seem at first sight. In almost every case good arguments exist against what people start out assuming to be true. By supplying arguments against widely held assumptions, philosophy can prevent people from falling into passionate errors and destructive falsehoods. In this way, Bertrand Russell suggested, philosophy, even when it fails to supply answers, can still inspire a way of life.

Index